ADVANCE PRAISE

I have been a Michelle Dobbins fan for a long time. I'm so glad she has graced the world with a missing piece of the puzzle. Law of Attraction works when our joy channels are open. Thanks, Michelle, for reminding us.

~Pam Grout
author of E-Squared, E-Cubed, and 15 other books
www.pamgrout.com

Michelle is not just a gifted writer, she's also the real deal when it comes to conscious creation. Her Personal Alchemy program is engaging, inspiring and fun to boot. Time in Michelle's world is time well spent!

~Jeannette Maw
The Good Vibe Coach & founder of Good Vibe University
www.goodvibeblog.com

In *Personal Alchemy*, Michelle Dobbins makes the art of manifestation approachable and fun. Filled with exercises we can do to raise our energy vibrations, *Personal Alchemy* can be used as a powerful tool to align ourselves with the life we desire. If you are confused about how to apply the Law of Attraction, and are ready to experience a life full of miracles, you must read this book.

~Cloris Kylie
author of Magnificent... Married or Not
www.cloriskylie.com

This super short, crystal clear book shines like a beacon from amongst the plethora of books about how to have a happy life. Michelle Martin Dobbins explores how each person has the power to use their 'personal alchemy' - not in order to make things happen; but in order to reconnect with our true, powerful selves. This is much more than some formulaic "do this and you'll be happy" set of instructions. In fact, Dobbins takes the whole "Law of Attraction" concept, picks it apart, shakes it up, gives it a thorough overhaul, adds in all the missing pieces - and finally puts it back together into a far broader, more inclusive and more powerful approach. Powerful, yes, but also eminently simple and do-able. This is also an entertaining read, with notes of humor, plenty of honesty about the author's own journey, and impeccable references. The kind of book I'll be keeping on my bedside for daily reference: highly recommended for veterans of deliberate creation and newbies alike. Alchemy, activate!

~Janette Dalgliesh
Brain Whisperer
www.youreverydaysuperpower.com

RELATIONSHIP
Alchemy

RELATIONSHIP
Alchemy

The Missing Ingredient to Heal
and Create Blissful Family,
Friendship, and Romantic
Relationships

MICHELLE MARTIN DOBBINS

ISBN 13: 978-1-942430-93-3
ISBN 10: 1-942430-93-0

 Year of the Book
135 Glen Avenue
Glen Rock, PA 17327

Front Cover Design: John Matthews

DEDICATION

*To my surrogate siblings,
Rosetta and Galen.*

*You two are the best cousins
an only child could have.*

TABLE OF CONTENTS

Chapter One:

What Is Alchemy?

He was 6'2" and magical. I adored him from the moment I met him. He enjoyed traveling and watching movies—just like me. We took long walks by the water, and then sat up all night talking about everything and nothing. I loved gazing into his hazel eyes. He owned his own business and he couldn't wait to take me on trips with him.

We were meant to be together and nothing could change that. I didn't even worry when he told me he had to take a business trip to the remote jungle of Belize and wouldn't be able to communicate with me while he was there. There was no internet and he would be working and living with the indigenous people, so he wanted to fit in and be a part of their culture while he was there. He'd have a local guide who spoke English and could get help if he needed it but he was sure he wouldn't. He would be away for up to a year.

We had settled into a lovely relationship and now he was leaving. Normally, I might have been distraught over someone I loved being away for such a long time, but our relationship was meant to be, and it would undoubtedly continue to improve once he returned from his journey. He had hinted at marriage, saying that when he came back, we could take our relationship to a deeper level. Although I was sad to see him go, it was important for his business, and moreover, I was secure in our relationship.

When he left, I walked around happy and engaged in my own life. I went camping with my friends, painted, had lunch by myself in little cafés, and read long novels. I was giddy and free. My lover would soon return. I no longer had to wonder how I looked to any potential date, no longer had anxiety or what-ifs, because I was already in my dream relationship. I would simply relax and enjoy life until he got back.

This story is fiction. In fact, it was the tale I told myself when I was single. I was a 25-year-old introverted, socially-awkward school teacher. My previous boyfriend had tried to kill himself multiple times. I took it personally, as though he wanted to leave the world rather than be with me, and did not think that boded well for my future happiness. I was mentally adrift and I was sure life would never go well for me again.

Luckily, the horrible spot I discovered myself in compelled me to search for a better way to live. I knew it must exist. My search first led to the Unity School of Christianity, a practical, positive-thought-oriented church. Then, my path developed to include yoga, the law of attraction, Reiki, meditation, and alchemy. All of these tools—and more—have totally changed my life.

Reverend Dick, at the Unity Church I attended, suggested I start living my own life as if I were already in a happy love relationship. That's how this story began. I told it to myself—every day—in detailed, elaborate versions. It made me excited about life. Even though the lover wasn't real, I did start living my life full out with passion. Did this mystery man ever appear in my life? I'll answer that question in detail in Chapter 4, but for now, let's dive into the topic of Relationship Alchemy.

What Is Alchemy, and How Can It Improve My Relationships?

First of all, I'm not an expert on relationships. Like you, I have been in relationships of various kinds all my life. Some of them were bad from the get-go, some full of ups and downs, and some divine. The divine ones have come about mostly in recent years, since I've learned more about relationship alchemy. If you are looking for a book that will teach you to communicate better with your spouse or how to have a fair argument with someone, this is not the book you are looking for.

Relationship alchemy is about shifting your relationships on a vibrational level. Of course, once you work on making those shifts, you will find you need to take some action to cement the changes you are creating in your relationships. I'll list a few good books that can help with those "real world" skills in the resources section at the end of the book because having that knowledge is helpful, too. If you have the combination of having your vibration aligned to what you want and know the practical steps to take, you can make even greater change.

Alchemy is the missing ingredient to allow the techniques from the other relationship books to work.

I'm also not an expert on alchemy. I have a Diploma in Alchemy from the Alchemy Study program, but I've barely scratched the surface of the wealth of knowledge in the spiritual realm. I've had a spiritual practice for over 20 years, and gradually learned what works for me and others.

Would I say my relationships are perfect? Far from it. My relationships are works-in-progress but they continue to improve and bring me innumerable moments of bliss. As I practice what I know, and focus on my own Personal Alchemy, everything in my life blossoms. I have been lucky enough to be married to my wonderful husband for the past 17 years. He has been the subject of many law of attraction experiments through the years and, luckily, they have only improved our relationship. I also have close relationships with most of my family members and often feel like my heart could burst from love when I sit around the dining room table with my husband and four children.

Even though, I am an introvert at heart, I still have friendships that have spanned over 40 years, and some newer ones that feel like I've known them for decades even though it's been only a few years. I occasionally have dramas with relationships and some that still haven't fully healed but I have the tools to shift them, when I'm ready. I'm going to share these tools with you so that you can improve all of your relationships as well.

What Is Alchemy?

Alchemy encompasses many things, and isn't easily defined. When most people think of alchemy, they envision an old man slaving away over beakers and a fire attempting to turn lead into gold. In truth, the historical alchemists were attempting to turn the leaden parts of themselves into gold—to raise their own energetic vibrations. The experiments they carried out were to speed up the transformation process, getting to the core essence of the substance they worked with and the core essences of themselves. They wanted to make their physical selves vibrate in harmony with their higher selves.

My favorite short and simple definition of alchemy is from Dennis William Hauck:

The art of transformation.

In my first book, Personal Alchemy, I discuss alchemy in depth and how it differs from the law of attraction. While raising your personal alchemy is helpful in all areas of your life, this book will give you all the information you need about relationship alchemy to artfully and radically transform your relationships. For now, here's all you need to know to get started:

1. Everything vibrates.

2. Higher (and faster) vibrations are attained when we go up the emotional scale. The happier we are, the higher we vibrate. Many different teachers have created emotional scales. My favorite is the one by David Hawkins, author of Power vs. Force. It starts at the bottom with shame, the lowest vibrating emotion, and then goes up through the emotions in this order: shame, guilt, apathy, grief, fear, desire, anger, pride, courage, neutrality, willingness, acceptance, reason, love, joy, peace, and enlightenment. The higher the emotion is on the scale, the higher it vibrates.

3. When we vibrate higher, our life and our relationships go smoother.

4. You can choose to raise your own vibration intentionally, and you'll learn lots of techniques in this book to do exactly that.

Relationship Alchemy is the art of transforming your relationships. That means creating, improving, and expanding our relationships—not only our love relationships but all of the relationships in our lives. Our relationships with family, friends, co-workers, and even strangers on the street can have a big impact on our life and happiness.

I've often heard people say, "Personal growth would be so easy, if it wasn't for other people." Actually, other people frequently spur us on to higher and deeper spiritual growth. Often, having conflict with others and a desire to create more authentic connections with them is what prompts us to begin the search for a way to improve our lives.

We all have a vibrational set point—that is, how we "normally" vibrate—which is approximately how happy we "normally" are. It can go up and down, but it usually returns to the set point, unless we make a conscious effort to raise our set point. It's similar in that way to our body weight. It may fluctuate, but we usually have a genetic set point. As with vibrations, our weight set point is not fixed either. Yet to create lasting change, we need to intentionally focus on it and take action to change.

Our relationships can't vibrate any higher than we do—for long. When we first meet someone we really care about, just being in their presence might raise our vibration, but over time we usually settle back down to our set point vibration. When we come together in a relationship, we create an entity (the relationship) that has its own vibration. It is a mix of the vibrations of people in the relationship.

Our relationships have their own essence, and the way we think about and treat them will affect their vibration. Since we are usually attracted to people with a similar vibration to our own, raising our vibration helps us attract people with whom we can have happier, more meaningful, and enjoyable relationships.

Strange as it may sound, our relationships take on a life of their own, like a book or business. We may write a book or create a business, but in time they have to develop their own energy and agenda. Although we created them, their energy is not the same as our energy.

I've heard musicians and visual artists say their art often takes on its own vibration. It's like they are guided in the creation, but the art becomes very much its own entity. Relationships are the same. They are more than just the sum of the vibrations of the people in them and sometimes they serve a higher purpose than we are necessarily aware of.

We also have vibrational set points in different areas of life and they may be relatively uneven.

Probably you've known someone who is very successful in business but can't keep a love relationship. Or maybe the opposite case—a person who has great relationships but struggles financially. In this book, we are going to focus on raising our set point around the subject of relationships. Still, many of the tools and thought shifts in this book can easily be applied to other parts of life (such as your relationships with money or success). My first book, *Personal Alchemy*, shares techniques to raise your core set point vibration, which will improve all areas of your life. I have often found that focusing on my vibration in one area of life effectively spills over and improves it in other areas, too.

Get ready! In the next chapters, we are going to re-frame and illuminate all of our relationships, from family relationships to love relationships and every connection in between.

BONUS!

Sign up and receive your free audio:

- What is the Difference Between Alchemy and Law of Attraction

dailyalchemy.com/relationship-alchemy

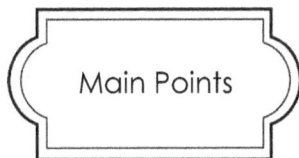

Main Points

- Alchemy is the "art of transformation."

- We all have a vibrational set point—one we can raise with intention and action.

- Our relationships each are their own entity, and have their own vibrations.

- When we raise our personal vibrations, the vibrations of our relationships rise and, accordingly, the relationships improve.

Chapter Two:

Using Alchemy to Heal & Improve Family Relationships

There I was, standing out in the rain, tears streaming down my face. Why? Because my date didn't show up? My boyfriend broke up with me? No, because my extended family didn't include me in an event. I felt betrayed, grief stricken, and guilty. I had messed up royally with my family relationships but did this mean I was going to be outcast for good?

I felt safe in my family being myself, and I was not always perfect. I did the wrong thing, said the wrong thing. I was guilty—and I hurt people. I shut them out, even though I loved them all very deeply. My family has caused me more pain than any lover ever has. They also said and did the "wrong" things and shut me out. They had brought me more love, joy, and acceptance than anyone else, too. My family, like most, holds dark secrets and sadness, pain, and addictions. It also holds joy and forgiveness and unconditional acceptance.

My family is closer than most, but not as close as others. We are tied together, even though we don't often talk about it. We come together often for family get-togethers, share food, some of us drink beer—and mingle souls.

My family is perfect. They make me cry, they make me laugh. They make me feel alive in the strangest of ways. Because we are all real. If you look at us from the outside, we may seem a motley crew. I know that each one of us is a link in a magical chain that supports us all throughout life. I adore my family, with all of its quirks and craziness.

I would trade it for nothing, but I would change it. I would fill it with love and I would uplift all those who have uplifted me throughout the generations. I would thank them for being a magic mirror that shows me where I need to change and grow, and I would reflect all their magnificence back to them.

"If you think you are enlightened, go spend a week with your family."

~Ram Dass

Families Are Magic

Families are our first relationships. We learn how to think and how to vibrate from our families. We wouldn't become who we are without our families. They are also, often, some of our most difficult relationships. When we improve these relationships, our whole lives tend to improve as well. It's worth the effort because the gains are incredible. Our family affects us so deeply that when we heal those relationships, often all those other seemingly unrelated problems—career, money, health— dissolve. By focusing on our family relationships, we have massively shifted our personal vibration and all facets of our lives are affected.

If your family relationships are too painful to deal with now, focus solely on raising your own personal alchemy and that will improve thoughts about your family and likely the relationships as well. Then, over time, you might feel more able to focus on your family relationships. Any area where we improve our vibrations and thoughts will spill over into other areas of our lives. Focusing on family relationships often enables big shifts because many of us have deeply rooted emotions and beliefs that can be healed when we heal our relationships with our family.

When you start to grow in your mother's womb, you are already soaking in her vibrations and the vibrations of all those around her who make up her world and affect her vibrations. Whether or not your father is around, he is part of the picture, too. His vibrations are imparted to you through his genetic matter that is helping to create your body. When we are born, we already recognize many people by their vibrations.

While it is true that your mother and father's DNA are the two main components that created you, their DNA is not theirs alone, it carries generations of genetic code passed on through the ages. As the genetic link is passed on, so are the vibrations. We mimic our family members as children. In doing so we match our vibrations to theirs and we learn the same thought patterns and stories about life. Usually we repeat them to ourselves and take them on as our own. We have to commit to strong intentions and action if we want to change our vibrations from the set patterns of our family.

Often times, when we discuss a disease as genetic, I wonder if it isn't more likely that it's vibrational. We pick up on the vibrations, beliefs, and stories our families tell, even before we are born. It may seem subtle, but through all of our childhood, we are soaking up and mimicking these family vibrations. They affect every facet of our lives.

Luckily, once we become aware we have control, we can change our vibrations intentionally. When we do that, we not only change our vibration, but science is now proving that we change our very DNA. In fact, Bruce Lipton, Ph.D, a stem cell biologist and bestselling author, discussed the difference between genetics and epigenetics, or "beyond" genetics.

> *The difference between these two is significant, because this fundamental belief called genetic determinism literally means that our lives, which are defined as our physical, physiological and emotional behavioral traits, are controlled by the genetic code.*

Lipton said in an interview with the online magazine, *Superconsciousness*, "This kind of belief system provides a visual picture of people being victims: if the genes control our life function, then our lives are being controlled by things outside of our ability to change them. This leads to victimization that the illnesses and diseases that run in families are propagated through the passing of genes associated with those attributes. Laboratory evidence shows this is not true."

We can change our lives, our DNA, and our family tree for the future. We don't live in a vacuum and all of our relationships can shift the world for the better—especially our family relationships. Perhaps changing our DNA is as easy as changing how we think. Some of you may have groaned out loud, believing it's difficult to change how you think. Some of us believe we can't control what we think. While it's true that thought seems to flit in and out of our mind with little rhyme or reason, there's one important element we have power over—which is the thoughts we focus on.

You may still hold your great-great-grandfather's vibrational pattern and his tendency toward bad knees. Now you can change that, not just for yourself, but for your whole family. Family alchemy can be a wonderful blessing. When one person rises, the whole family as a collective will rise. Maybe the opposite is true to a certain extent, as when one person sinks, but I do not believe we have to be victim to that if we are aware of our own vibrational energies. Also, higher vibrations are so much stronger than lower ones. That one person in a family raising their vibrations can positively affect the family as a whole.

Do Families Really Matter that Much?

Family matters first. You are energetically linked to them, but if your family set point is lower than you wish, that doesn't mean they hold power over you—or that they can hold your vibration down indefinitely. What it does mean, is that they are a group of people who you can potentially bless when you raise your own vibration. When we uplift our personal vibration, the whole planet benefits, but our family benefits the most because there is a stronger energetic bond.

It's also important to be aware of your family alchemy, because you were most likely raised around those vibrations and those stories. Even if you weren't raised around your biological family, you still have those vibrations encoded in your DNA. If you don't know your family of origin, their vibration won't affect you as much. In that case, I would intend and affirm that I only receive the best and higher vibrations from their DNA and that my body will transmute any generational negativity. Take care not to interpret this to mean that your family is an energetic "disability" or something that is difficult to overcome. Awareness is the biggest key to shifting it. We can create our own destiny. We can use alchemy to raise our vibrations.

The Kennedys are said by some to be "cursed," so many people in their family die young—and tragically. However, many people in their family are also wealthy, influential, and successful. It's not a curse that hurts them, it is family vibrations that are passed down, but each member of the family can choose whether or not to continue to vibrate those stories. If they chose not to, then I believe the family vibrations will begin to subtly shift—benefitting the whole family.

You Don't Understand How Bad My Family Is...

I've heard a few times, "My family is worse than you can

imagine. They are all horrible and awful people."
Actually, your family is a gift, even if it's a gift that you
might prefer to return or re-gift to the creepy guy in
your office. Sometimes the gift is supportive, nurturing
people. Sometimes the gift is in getting thrown out of
the nest to grow and choose a path of your own.
Sometimes the gift might be hard to see, but it's there.
And not only this, it's the perfect size for you. Maybe the
gift is that it compels you to decide that now that you
are grown, you are going to focus on vibrating totally
differently than you were taught and you may thereby
become happier and more successful than if your family
"set point" had not been dissatisfying.

If you family is truly dangerous for your body and soul,
it is perfectly fine and sometimes advisable to cut
physical ties with them. I would suggest, however, that
you continue to connect with the higher selves of your
earthly family. In that way, they can still support you,
and you can realize gifts from your family. If this is your
circumstance, don't skip this chapter. Keep reading, and
decide if the exercises are right for you.

Please, don't think I'm saying it's "OK" if you were
abused or neglected, but at this point, remember, you
get to decide where to go from here. You get to choose
how you develop your own life and how you vibrate. You
get to seek out love and healing in the way that works
for you. Often that includes forgiveness—not for their
benefit, but for you—so you can let go of pain and focus
on creating a life you love.

We are never irrevocably damaged. Bodies can be
damaged enough that they can no longer live, but your

spirit and your soul will always heal. Follow your heart and do what it tells you is best. I believe there is a part of us that never dies and is not capable of evil, even if our human form is. That is the higher self and it is the part of your family members that you can reach out to, even if you never want to reach out to them in present form. If that message speaks to you, heal your relationship with their higher selves. If it doesn't, focus on healing yourself and create your own new "family."

What If I Don't Have a Family?

The short answer is: You do! Even if you were abandoned at birth and spent your entire life in an orphanage, you have a biological family by virtue of your birth. You are energetically tied to the birth family, even if you never met any of them. You are also free to create your own family now—and the bonds you form can grow to be just as powerful as the bond with your family of origin.

You can create family ties and love. This is a gift that is denied no one. We are all related somehow, so if you have no biological family in your life right now, lucky you—you get to create one intentionally. Once we get to the exercises, we will all get to create a family we love, but if you are starting with a blank canvas, you actually have a lot of power to create a joyous family alchemy.

Parent Alchemy

Our parents are the people who often affect our vibrations the most. Some of us have only one parent and some of us have more than two. It's a deep bond, especially when they raise us. We inherit the vibrations from their DNA, and we are exposed to those vibrations on a daily basis throughout our childhood.

This is excellent news for one of two reasons. If you have wonderful relationships with your parents, chances are good that the rest of your life is going pretty well, especially if they have a strong vibration and personal alchemy that they passed on to you. If your relationship with your parents isn't (or wasn't) good and you don't think they passed on the best vibrations for creating a happy life, then once you work on shifting your relationship with them and take control of your own vibration, miracles can happen.

One friend, "Mary," thought she had the worst childhood ever and couldn't even stand to be in the same room with her mother. Mary decided to work on some of these exercises and specifically open her heart to love her mother more. As she raised her own vibration, she blessed her mother and sent her love. In turn, Mary's mother began to call more. Not only that, as they grew closer, she couldn't even remember why she thought her childhood was so bad. Once her relationship with her mother had healed—creating a whole new relationship alchemy—Mary went on to double her income in less than six months. All the energy tied up in hating her mother was set free, where she could use it to improve her life, instead of allowing it to effectively lower her personal vibration.

If you do this work and things don't seem any different when you interact with your parents, yet you feel better about them and about the relationship, you have succeeded. Things often do shift because, on an unconscious level, they can feel the work you have done and the change in the relationship alchemy.

Even if they don't perceive a shift or behave any differently, it doesn't mean the work wasn't worth doing. The positive changes you have created—energy invested—will come back to you somewhere, even if it's not through that relationship.

What About Our Children?

Improving the relationships with our children and helping them grow up with the highest and truest vibrations for themselves, is a subject for a whole other book. I'm not going to say too much about our relationships with our own children in this book but I will tell you two things that I consider of the highest importance in fostering the best relationship alchemy possible with our children as they grow.

The first is to work on your own personal alchemy. Children don't simply listen to what we tell them to do. They feel the vibrations behind our words and even actions. They know who we are at our core and that is what they usually mimic. If you want to raise happy children who know their own worth and love themselves—your number one priority is to be happy, know your worth, and love yourself. I have seen so many well-meaning parents give excessively to their children and sacrifice their own self-care, then not understand why their children don't feel love that their parents are trying to give them.

Children can feel the vibration of parents actually withholding love from themselves and so they copy them and in turn withhold love from themselves. It's such a sad cycle and this gets passed through generations without our realizing it. If you don't feel like you deserve to give yourself love, do it for your children! You deserve it and it will benefit them as much as it benefits you.

The second is to trust your children. Trust that they know who they are and what they want out of life. They "come in" knowing this information and as long as we haven't trained it out of them or modeled for them not to trust their inner guidance, they know. Love them for who they are. Don't try to make them into something they did not choose. Remember, they are already unconsciously vibrating like you. Often times, I think each generation is born with more knowledge and achievement coded into their DNA. They know it is their job to make the world better and it is our job to step back and let them. So guide your kids and keep them safe but be aware that they may already know more about how the world is meant to be than we do—so let them grow and discover how to create it.

Exercises to Improve Your Family Alchemy

Remember, you now get to choose what to believe about your family and the relationships in it. You can decide that you are at a disadvantage because of your family, or you can tell a story about your family that feels good. We can all go either way. You can tell yourself about the hardship making you stronger. You can tell yourself how having high-vibrating relatives made the path easier for you. Or you can tell the opposite. If your family relationships aren't exactly how you want them to be, here are some exercises to help improve your family alchemy:

Family DNA Vibe Healing

As we have discussed, we can change our personal vibration, and perhaps literally change our DNA, by changing our thought patterns. I believe that we can change this not just for ourselves, but for future generations—and some might even say for past generations. I like to do this simple meditation to heal past negative thoughts and raise my families' vibration. (If you prefer to listen, there is a link to an audio version on this webpage: dailyalchemy.com/relationship-alchemy.)

You can modify this and make it your own:

> First, take a moment to breathe and relax your body. Know that the spirits of all members of your family, whether known to you or not, stand with you. They are here to help heal and clear past history and give all members freedom to create their own paths.

> Imagine, in your mind's eye, a huge tree with massive roots. Roots that reach all the way to the center of the earth, and limbs that rise up to touch the clouds. The family that you are a part of goes on forever. It was meant to support you, not tear you down.

> Take a moment, and stand back to look at the tree. Do you see any areas of weakness? Any areas where

there appears to be disease on the bark or holes where it has been munched on by animals?

Send healing thoughts to the tree. Invite all of your ancestors, current family members, and future family members to send healing as well. Watch as the tree gets stronger and healthier. Keep sending healing thoughts, until the tree looks strong and healthy.

Imagine the tree's DNA, and imagine it whole and strong. Imagine that any limiting qualities are immediately and permanently healed. Feel the tree's vibration. Feel the strong, high vibrations it now emanates. It is there to support you, not to control you.

Imagine sitting under the tree and leaning back against it trunk. Let it support you and pass its healing on to you. Feeling its healing strength soaking into your body and raising its vibrations. Mother Earth supports your family tree and in turn they both support you.

Sit and rest under the tree, taking in the healing from the earth you sit on and from the tree you rest against. Sit quietly until you feel the energy shift. The healing is complete and it will change not only you, but any member of your family who, consciously or unconsciously, chooses to shift too.

You may decide to do this only once, or you can do it more often if you feel the desire for additional healing.

Blessing Your Family

I learned about blessing people and situations many years ago though Catherine Ponder in her book, *The Prosperity Secrets of the Ages*. The practice has served me well over the years and it can be wonderful to do for your family. It is a very simple way to say a positive prayer for someone or something. One of Catherine Ponder's favorites is, "I bless you, and bless you for the goodness of god that is within you." You can create your own blessings, just like you create your own affirmations.

In so doing, we are not trying to change someone to our will but to offer our positive thoughts of good for them. When you are sending positive thoughts and vibrations toward a person, they are much more likely to respond in kind. It always has much better results than cursing them. Emmet Fox, the author of *The Golden Key to Prayer*, said:

> Bless a thing and it will bless you. Curse a thing and it will curse you. If you put your condemnation upon anything in life, it will hit back at you and hurt you. If you bless a situation, it has no power to hurt you and even if it is troublesome for a time, it will gradually fade out, if you sincerely bless it.

I always try to remember that happy people aren't mean or rude, so I send my blessings to those who treat others cruelly. If they become happy, they will change their behavior. In turn we all benefit, especially when they are our family members. Even if things don't spontaneously shift with the person or situation being blessed, you will feel better once you have been able to bless them, as it is a high vibration intention and it releases negative feelings.

When it comes to family, you can just randomly bless any family member who comes into your thoughts or you can create a list either online or in a notebook. I have a list that also includes my ancestors and I keep it in my blessing book, a notebook that has lists of people I might want to send blessings to. You can ask that all on the list be blessed, which I normally do and then I usually ask if there is someone who needs an additional blessing to please make it known to me. Then, if a person's face or name pops into my mind or my eyes land on a name, I speak an additional blessing for them and send them energy healing, whether they are alive or not.

My cousin does genealogy work, and she says she can feel the spirits of our ancestors wanting to tell their story and experience the blessing of being known to future generations. It can also be a nice way to connect to your family tree, and you can intentionally raise family vibrations in the process.

Creating Your Own Family

Even if we don't know our family of origin, or maybe we do and choose not to belong, we can still create our own. By the time we are adults, most of us have a family of some kind. We may have been adopted or in a long-term fostering situation, but most of grew up in a family environment. Even if you aren't related to that family by blood, you still have been surrounded by their vibration and may have even shifted your DNA to resemble theirs. Also, the principle of "like attracts like" applies, so we grew up with the right people for us—whether they were "blood" related or not.

Now that you are grown up, if you want to improve your family alchemy, you can create new positive stories about the people in that family. If you don't have a family, or you want to add people to yours, you can create new stories about them, too. We will create stories of events we wish would have happened or improved versions of events that did happen. Really, we aren't "remembering" the actual events anyway, but our interpretation of them, so we might as well articulate them in the best way we can. We will also write biographies of family members as we wish them to be. You can also make up a family member that doesn't exist, but who you would like to have in your family.

When I did this, I started with a nice journal and somewhere labeled it, "Michelle Martin Dobbins' Family History: This or Something Better for the Highest Good of all the Family Members." I didn't want to create my family in a way that would take anything away from each other's uniqueness and free will.

I started with the biographies of the family members I knew and I wrote the best version of them that I could imagine. Then, I wrote the stories from my childhood that I wanted to change and I made a new and improved version of events. I also made up events and people that didn't exist and put them in there.

I go back through my family tree and write stories about the people who lived in my family before I was born. I write about events that I would love to see occur in the future. If you've heard of pray rain journaling, this is a family history version of this. The funny thing is, the more I did this the more I loved my actual family tree. It also seemed that some events healed and I now remember them the way they were in my created family history, while some still exist in the way they happened in fact—but my feelings about them have changed. As with most thought work, I would take care not to show your personal journal to anyone, especially family members, as it can be readily misunderstood. This is for you and your personal growth. It can positively affect your family alchemy, but that won't happen if someone else reads it and doesn't like what they read.

Family Alchemy for Raising Your Vibration

Whether you already feel that your family tree has a strong vibration, or you've done healing work to create it that way, your family alchemy can be a great tool for raising your own vibration. If you have learned to feel your own vibration and feel the vibrations of people or places, this will be helpful. If you haven't learned this skill, there is a free eKit on my website dailyalchemy.com/get-your-happy-back, that will teach you to perceive vibration. I would follow those steps and tap into the vibration of your family tree like you did when you did the Family DNA Vibe healing exercise.

Once you are visualizing yourself sitting under your family tree and feeling the strong vibrations, ask your family members past and present to help you raise your vibration to the family vibrations. If there is a skill or a talent you would like to develop, ask any family members who already possess that skill to transfer the vibrations of it to you. Offer to share your knowledge and higher-vibration areas with the rest of the family.

Use the session to support and be supported. You can imagine that in all your family history, there is probably someone who is better than you at the skills you wish to learn and they can help pass this knowledge onto you. Don't forget to include future family members, too. You can send this energy into the future, and indeed by shifting your beliefs, you can improve the vibration that is passed onto future generations. Even though this is a visualization, the results can be very powerful.

BONUS!

Sign up and receive your free audio:

- Family DNA Vibe Healing Meditation

dailyalchemy.com/relationship-alchemy

Main Points

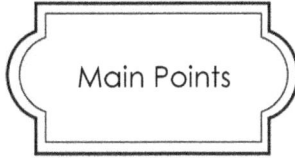

- Families are powerful magic. When you improve the vibration of your relationship with your family's family, all areas of your life will usually improve.

- Not only do we inherit DNA, but we internalize vibrational levels from our family.

- We can change not only our personal vibrations, but we may even heal our DNA or change the way it is expressed.

- Even "bad" families are gifts, guiding us as we grow and develop our own lives.

- We get to tell our own story of our family's effect on us, so we might want to focus on telling a positive story. Healing our thoughts about our family, especially our parents, can heal our whole lives.

- The most important thing we can do for our children is to love and care for ourselves, because they will mimic our self-love and self-care automatically.

- We need to trust our children and thereby teach them to trust and follow their own inner guidance.

- You can improve your family alchemy with the help of the spirits and higher selves of all your family members, past, present, and future.

Chapter Three:

Using Relationship Alchemy to Create and Improve Friendships

In September of 1999, I cried for a week when I didn't go back to work with all of my friends. I had been a teacher in Richmond County for seven years, and for the past four, I had worked out of an office of about 30 traveling teachers. Many of us were very close, having lunch together and going out on the weekends. We were bonded because of our common job, so although I did remain close friends with several of these ladies, I was correct in anticipating that these friendships would not be the same now that I was no longer part of the sorority of teachers.

I was 6 months pregnant and alone much of the time then, working from home, answering the phones and doing the accounting for my husband's business. I was thrilled that I wouldn't have to put my baby in daycare, but the reality was that I was alone most of the time. My husband was out in the field working many hours to keep our new heating and cooling business afloat. Once my daughter was born in December, I was even more isolated. Luckily, her birth coincided with the hire of a full-time secretary for our office, so I was no longer chained to our house all day for the business.

For the first time in my life, I set out to create a friendship intentionally. Most of my friendships just happened circumstantially, because I spent time in proximity to a certain person, or shared a significant experience. I worked with them; I went to school with them, etc. By this time in my life, though, I knew that I could create my own reality and I wanted to make a friend.

I made a list of the qualities I wanted this friend to have, and I meditated on what it would feel like to spend time with this friend. Then, I went on about my life. A week or so later, I felt led to go to a yoga class at the Unity Church. I didn't have a babysitter, but I called and asked if the teacher would mind if I brought my baby. That was totally out of character for me, but I felt prompted to do it. The day I met Sharada, the yoga teacher, I knew she was the friend I had wanted to attract. I went to yoga several times a week after that, and I brought my daughter with me. Many times it was just us in the class and we would chat and have lunch together afterward. We ended up traveling together and doing so many fun things.

If you had asked me if I thought I would be able, as a young mother, to take off and go to yoga retreats in Florida and Ohio with my friend, I wouldn't have logically thought it possible. Once I let go of my stories and logic, and just felt the joy of what kind of friend I wanted, it brought all kinds of magic into my life. Over the years and many moves, our friendship has evolved. I can still talk to Sharada on the phone, and it's like I just saw her yesterday. She was the first friend I intentionally attracted, and the first friendship I had in which I noticed that we created a vortex together, which raised one another's vibration.

Why Friends Matter

Unlike our families, we get to choose our friends. However, when we look back at our own friendships through the years, it may not seem that way for all of us. Many of us "choose" friends who vibrate and behave similarly to our own family's vibration.

A study published recently by researchers in *Proceedings of the National Academy of Science*, found that people are apt to pick friends who are genetically similar to themselves. In fact, friends tend to be as genetically similar to each other as a pair of fourth cousins. The researcher hypothesized that it had something to do with our sense of smell, but I'll wager it has more to do with similar vibrational patterns. This is comfortable for us. We are used to our family's vibration, but it still doesn't necessarily mean it's our best choice. The wonderful thing is, as we raise our own vibration, our current friendships improve or dissolve, and we attract friends who are a better match for the person we have become. This is parallel to what can happen with family.

Friendships can become as strong as, or stronger than family bonds. Many of them last throughout the generations, too. Friendships are a wonderful way to raise our vibration, especially when two or more people come together for the purpose of enjoying life or improving the world. Spiritual people may think friendships aren't important, but time spent doing activities you love with people you love is a great way to raise your vibration.

> "Again I say to you that if two of you agree on earth concerning anything that they ask, it will be done for them by My Father in heaven. For where two or three are gathered together in My name, I am there in the midst of them." (Matthew 18:19–20, NKJV)

When I think of this passage from the Bible, it reminds me that we are more together than we are apart. Our relationships not only bring us joy, they can bring us personal growth and they can even raise the vibration of our planet. Whether we work together in partnership or simply support each other's growth, friendships are magic. If your friendships don't feel magical, and they aren't bringing you the joy you want, look through some of these exercises and see if they might help you create friendships that truly support you.

It doesn't matter how many friends you have. It matters how your friendships feel to you. Friendships can be like possessions: too many can weigh you down and become a burden, instead of an uplifting association. In school, many of us believed that being popular was important. Hopefully, over time, we learn that true connections with other people are more important.

I'm naturally introverted, so I'm most content with a few close friendships—and several acquaintances who I don't have to feel so strongly tied to. If you are an extrovert, more friends may feed your energy and not drain it. Pay attention to the relationship alchemy of your friendships—how they make you feel. If they are uplifting, continue them. If not, then either pull back from them or focus on changing the alchemy of the relationship by working through some of the exercises below.

Do friendships your own way

Here again, family patterns may be influencing us. We might have the same type of friends that our family members had, and do the same types of things with our friends that they did with theirs. Now that we are aware this happens and that we have more choices, we can set our own intentions about the friendships we want to create.

You can even make a list of the kinds of friendships you want to have. Maybe you ride horses, shoot skeet, play golf or have some other hobby and you want a friend who will enjoy these hobbies with you. This person doesn't need to have anything more in common with you than the love of the shared activity.

You can create so many different types of relationships. The only rule I have for friendships is that over time, the alchemy of the relationship should rise and we should support each other's personal growth. That does not mean that you ever have to say the word alchemy, or even speak of anything about spirituality or the law of attraction with your friend. If you both enjoy riding horses together, that is enough to raise both of your vibrations. Shared positive experiences and joy will raise your relationship vibration and your individual vibrations as well.

For most of us, usually only one or two of our friendships will be the kind of friends with whom you sit and talk about deep subjects at length. Not because you are uncomfortable talking about those subjects with certain people, but just that the joy in some relationships comes from shared activities, which might be pure fun or service. Taking shared action toward a common goal, even and especially if that goal is just to enjoy life, is the key.

Often, spiritual people, myself sometimes included, spend too much time thinking and talking about improving their lives, when they should be out in the world living it. Those are the best friendships—the ones where the place they begin and you end is "lost" temporarily in the joy of living the same passions at the same time. It's a feeling we commonly associate with lovers, but can be a part of the closest of friendships, too.

Take the time to let go and just be with your friends and deeply connect to your shared activities. You'll find it creates massive growth, and all it takes is being in the moment and sharing joy with another person. So much better, vibrationally, than sitting in therapy and talking about your problems for hours!

You might make a list of the ways you want to connect with friends, and ways that you wish to support your friends. Some friends might just fit into one category, while others might hold many. You can have hobby sharing friends, travel friends, party friends, eating out friends, mommy friends, creative friends, etc. Everyone also needs at least one "It's 2 AM and I need someone to talk to friend." It happens rarely, once we focus on getting happy, but we all have those moments and need a friend who doesn't mind being woken up in the wee hours to lend support. Just make sure you are that friend for someone, too.

If a friend starts to make you uncomfortable, needs more than you want to give, or creates too much drama in your life, it's OK for you to drop them. I suggest doing it with love. It's nice to gently let them know that your schedule has changed and you don't have time to do the activities you once did together. If necessary, you may want to tell them gently why you are cutting the ties. As I said, I'm not a relationship expert, but I would do what is the kindest act for them. Maybe they need to know and maybe they don't. If it's just that their vibration doesn't feel harmonious to you, there's no need to share that information. If they are behaving in a way that may cost them other friendships, then it may honestly benefit them to let them know. If so, do it in a way that supports their growth, which generally produces minimal drama for everyone.

Bring new life to an old friendship, or create a new one

All relationships change and grow over time, especially friendships. We may make changes in our lifestyle, or move to a new city, and not see one another as often. We may drop a hobby and end up curtailing a friendship along with it. If you have a friendship that you miss, there are two ways to get that energy back into your life. One is to re-kindle the friendship. The other is to create a relationship with a similar vibration, with a new friend. Don't sit back and lament the beloved friendship that has gone awry or that just faded for no apparent reason. You can create the same feelings now. If you feel you want to create it with that particular friend and you've lost contact, or had hard feelings between you, try connecting with their higher self to open the possibility. Here's a link to a free audio that will lead you through this process: dailyalchemy.com/relationship-alchemy.

After you have connected with their higher self, follow your intuition on whether or not to contact them, if you are even able to, or to let them come to you. I use this technique often. While I don't always see results, I usually do. I've reconnected with lost friends that I knew no way to contact, within weeks of doing this process. I've also experienced some relationships healing themselves, just by doing this process. Sometimes, nothing happens—so I let it go and create a new relationship. Knowing that, for the lost one to maybe come back some day, it's more likely to happen when I'm relaxed about it.

If you'd like to create a new relationship with a similar vibration, I would suggest visualizing the best times you had in the original friendship. Create and experience the feelings you had when you spent time together. Remember the sights, smell, tastes, and surroundings, and some of your most special memories. Then, set your intention to enjoy more of this.

If visualizing is hard for you, or you want to focus deeper, writing new stories can serve this purpose well. Start journaling out stories of your old friendship, and then write some new stories about the new friendship you are creating in present tense—explaining how similar they are, and how they both fill the same need for your soul. Then, relax and let it go—know that it is coming. Don't work at it, but do follow your feelings and intuitive prompts. If you see a class that speaks to you, take it. If you feel urged to go to a party, go. If you see someone interesting, speak to them. Do take action toward your goal, but make it light and easy actions.

How to attract new and satisfying friendships

Even if you aren't looking for a friendship to replace one that you lost, you may want to create a new and different relationship in your life. Look around for a model friendship. Maybe some people you know have a friendship that has the energy you want to create, or you can look for a model friendship from famous people, literature, or television.

Here are a few friendships that might inspire you: Ben Affleck and Matt Damon (who have been friends since childhood); Patrick Stewart and Ian McKellen (Google their names and friendship and you'll smile at all the cool stuff they have done together); Tina Fey and Amy Poehler (funniest friends ever); Oprah and Gayle King (friends through thick and thin); Gertrude Stein and Ernest Hemingway (creative friends who helped inspire each other's writing); Lewis and Clark (exploring friends); Scooby and Shaggy (best friends forever).

There are so many to choose from—and you can pick more than one. Ultimately, every friendship has its own energy, but focusing on the type you want to experience will help you create it.

Once you have decided what type of friendship you want, and can tune into the energy you wish it to have, start telling the story of your friendship the way you want it to be. Stop telling the old stories that limit your experience. Stop telling yourself that men can't be friends with women. Stop telling yourself that all the women you know are catty. Stop telling yourself that those kinds of friendships only exist on TV. Stop telling yourself any story that doesn't support what you are creating for your future. Write out the new stories about the wonderful friendships you are enjoying instead. Write it in present tense as if it's already happening, and then go out and live as though it's already happening, while making room for friendships in your life.

Make time for friendships

Life moves fast for many of us, and now that we have all kinds of electrical gadgets, we don't always take the time to sit and talk with people in person, or make time for dinners and fun activities with friends. If you are like me and you have young children, it can be even harder to find time for actual friends. You can have online relationships, but take the time to also connect with people in the "real" world. It is so powerful to mingle our energy with others, creating a new vibration from that mixing that blesses us all. Our relationships, our friendships, and our partnerships can actually impact the world.

So, make time for your friends. Put them on your calendar. Schedule "friend playdates" for the month, just as you schedule your other appointments and then, fill them. If you are waiting to make new friends, still make the open appointments and write in them what you would like to do with a friend. Making the space in your life, and in real time, for a new friendship lets the universe know that you are serious and you are ready to create relationships. Consider even going and doing the ideal event by yourself, if you can. Go to the movies or hiking or whatever by yourself. You might just meet that new friend when you are there.

If your friendships don't feel magical, and they aren't bringing you the joy you want, try some of these exercises and see if they help you create friendships that support you.

Exercises

1. Friendship Band-Aid

This exercise is for a friendship that has gone awry. One that hurts your heart to think about and you want to heal it. It also works for any other type of relationship on the rocks.

1) *Set your intention to raise the alchemy of the relationship and heal it.* Be aware that healing takes place on an energetic level; it may or may not change how the relationship appears on the physical plane. Plan to be OK, no matter the outcome, and know that the healing has occurred, whether or not anything changes.

Think big. You are already impacting the world every single day. You might as well decide how you want to do it.

2) Decide, in your opinion, whose fault it was that the relationship foundered. Just so you know, if two parties are involved, then there are two people at fault. For this exercise, if you feel it was their fault, complete number 3. If you believe it was your fault, complete number 4. If you know both of your actions or attitudes were involved, complete both steps. At some point you may decide to do both anyway, but follow your intuition for now.

3) If you believe the other person was at fault, make a list of what the other person did to you that you think was wrong. Then turn your focus around, and give yourself what you think they withheld from you. If you think they didn't respect you, give yourself respect. If they weren't honest with you, be honest with yourself. If they acted like they didn't care, take time to care for yourself. It is important that these be real actions. DO NOT just do this in your head with thought alone. Take at least two actions that essentially give yourself what you believed were missing from the friend. Once you feel that you have received what you needed from yourself, you might want to use the exercise to connect with their higher self from earlier in the chapter and offer your forgiveness. We have a hard time receiving from others what we will not allow ourselves to have. People cannot show up in our

lives and give us what we withhold from ourselves. We have to be able to accept what we want people to offer.

4) If you believe you are at fault for the relationship's problems, make a list of the reasons you feel you are at fault, and follow the steps above. Give yourself the things you withheld from the other person. Then take action in an attempt to give what you withheld to the person you hurt. If that's not possible, give them to some other person in their place. Finally, connect with the friend's higher self and ask for forgiveness. I like to visualize myself bowing and laying a bouquet of peace lilies at their feet. Sometimes, I will visualize myself hugging the other person, feeling the relief that the relationship is healed.

It may seem strange to focus so much on giving what was withheld to yourself, but I find that is usually the root of the problem. We believe we don't deserve respect, love, honestly, fidelity, etc. and we withhold it from ourselves, and in turn, it is hard for us to receive it from others—or for others to feel comfortable giving it to us.

2. Friendship Vortex

Abraham-Hicks wrote a book called *The Vortex: Where the Law of Attraction Assembles All Cooperative Relationships*. It is a fabulous read and inspires me to do a meditation and visualization when I want to improve or create friend relationships. According to

Abraham-Hicks, all of our relationships, with everyone and everything that we desire, already exist in the vortex —and all we have to do is line up with them. I totally agree and the friendship vortex is one of the ways I like to line up with that energy.

The meditation and visualization I use are simple. First, I sit down and relax and feel my own vibration. For me, just focusing on the sensation of my vibration causes it to rise. You can start with whatever technique gets you into a relaxed state. Then, I think of words, colors, feelings, smells, sensations, and experiences that remind me of what I want to create. For example, you might see the words *joy*, *love of horses*, *connection*, *conversation*, etc. You might see these words in certain colors or just see a certain color swirling about. Try to focus on feeling the emotion you want the new friendship to create. If you want to create a golf buddy, you might smell the fresh cut grass on the golf course or hear the swing of the clubs. Then, mentally tag or pin these sensory placeholders to yourself, and enter the "vortex."

To me, being in the vortex is like being in a tornado of love. I feel spinning, whirling, love energy around me, like I'm standing in a totally safe tornado made up of all the energy of everyone I could possibly be friends with. I intend that my energy will match with the energy of people who have these tagged experience placeholders in common with me. I can see them lighting up in the tornado as they spin around me, but I don't try to figure out what they look like or who they actually are. I just allow our energies to connect. I see strands of energy connecting out to others in the tornado and I know that

I will connect with them in my physical reality when the time is right. I continue to let this visualization flow in my mind, until the tornado starts to slow down and feels complete. I complete the meditation by giving thanks that all the relationships I desire are already vibrationally connected and that I will manifest them in that perfect time.

BONUS!

Sign up and receive your free audio:

- The Friendship Vortex

dailyalchemy.com/relationship-alchemy

Main Points

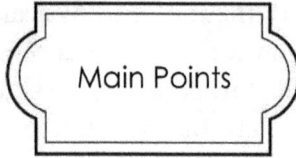

- Even though we get to choose our friends in life, we often choose people who vibrate in a way similar to our family.

- The number of our friends is not as important as the energy of our friendships.

- Make time and space for your friends, even for the ones you haven't met yet.

- Our friendships, and the relationship alchemy from them, can change the world.

- Choose to have the kind, number, and combination of friendships that feels most joyful to you.

Chapter Four:

Using Alchemy to Attract a Significant Other

I knew my husband was the man I would marry within a week of meeting him, maybe sooner. He fit almost all of the characteristics of my list of the ideal mate, but more importantly, I felt a vibration from him that matched what I felt when I told the story of my love from the first chapter of the book. As I told that story— about knowing I already had a wonderful relationship —I began to feel the energy of the vibration, learned the feeling of my ideal relationship, and recognized it as soon as I felt it in "real" life. I told the story about six months before I met him, so I had practiced the feeling until I knew it thoroughly.

He didn't fit the entire story I had told about my love at the beginning of the book, but he felt familiar, like the vibration of it. He hadn't traveled out of the country, but had been here all along. It seems that I needed to relax and raise my vibration before I could meet him. We had nearly met each other several times, but as I like to believe, it didn't happen in real life until our vibrations were both ready. He had recently begun planning to start his own business and he was magical with animals. There were times when I wasn't sure he was the right person because we were so different. Yet every sign I asked for confirmed he was indeed right.

My questions came primarily from other people's thoughts and my mind. My heart and my soul felt that his vibration was the one I was looking for. Now I know that he has qualities that make our relationship work. I had wanted someone spiritual like me, but he is actually very practical, and he deals with all of the things that I don't like to deal with—and vice versa. Sometimes, what we think we want isn't the choice that will actually make us happy. I'm glad I focused on matching up with the feeling, instead of insisting on a list of qualities I wanted in a man. Letting the universe work some magic made things come out even better than I could have dreamed.

In the beginning of the book, I described how I started telling myself the story of my relationship that wasn't real, yet. By creating this story of my love, who was temporarily away from me, I was able to relax and enjoy my life without feeling desperate to meet someone. Once I was happy and engaged in my own life, I became much more attractive to the opposite sex. If you are looking for your life partner, I can't tell you enough how important it is to get happy now, before you find a partner. If you don't, you may not like what you attract.

Romantic relationships are the type of relationships that are most possible to go through life without, but often the kind we crave the most. We want deep intimacy with someone. However, if you don't have that deep connection with yourself first, it's very hard to establish it with another person.

If you recently ended a relationship, or if you feel like you are struggling to find a relationship and becoming lonely and desperate, take some time to work on your own personal alchemy before you press for a new relationship. Don't rush into a new relationship if you have a broken heart. Take time to let your heart heal and allow your vibration to rise. If you jump too quickly into a relationship, while you are still vibrating heartbreak, it's less likely you will attract and sustain a happy relationship. Get happy and let the relationship come to you.

If you find it difficult to let go of thinking about finding someone, do what I did and tell the story of how your love is away from you for a good reason and wants you to be happy and enjoying your life until you are reunited. This helps in two ways. First, it frees you up to move forward and enjoy life without frantically seeking new love. Secondly, it helps you achieve a vibration of "having" a relationship, which is what will actually bring you the kind of relationship you want. If you are matched up with the vibration of "having" a relationship, it is much easier to manifest one than it is when you are holding the vibration of "wanting" a relationship. That just keeps you in the position of wanting.

Don't worry that you are going to miss "the one," or that you have already missed "the one." I have some friends who were born far apart, then narrowly missed meeting each other several times when they were at the same conferences, but they still ended up together in the same graduate program, surprised by how many times they were in the same room together over the years yet had never met. They have now been married for 20 years, so waiting 4 or 5 years didn't seem to hurt their relationship at all. Plus, there is more than one potential mate for you.

I once knew a man who told all of the girls he dated that he had met the one true love of his life and lost her. Therefore, he said, he would enjoy dating them, but they needed to know upfront that he would never love them and he was never going to get married, because no one else could ever measure up. You're probably not shocked that his relationships never lasted and he didn't get a lot of second dates. Everything he believed was hogwash. If he was truly meant to be with that woman, he would have been with her. He needed to start telling new stories about how he created an even better relationship with someone he adored. Many of us do this, too. If we have broken up with or divorced someone we cherished, it's hard to believe that we can have a wonderful relationship again. We can! We can create anything we believe we deserve.

What Stories Are You Telling About Your Relationships?

If you haven't created a romantic relationship that brings you joy, take some time to comb through your thoughts and think about what you say and think about your relationships and what underlies those statements or opinions. Do you, or does your inner critic, say or think anything like:

- There are no good guys (or girls) left.

- I'll never find the person I want to marry.

- Relationships never last anyway.

- I'm too old to find a new love.

- I weigh too much to find someone to love me.

- I'm too shy to ask someone out.

- I lost my one true love.

- I don't have enough money to attract a woman.

- I'm not good-looking enough to attract someone I'd want to date.

If the story you are telling about relationships isn't positive, stop telling it. You might enjoy even being self-deprecating about relationships with your friends or family members, but telling these stories is actually creating a belief that you don't want to have. Tell positive stories. Look at people who have magical relationships and say to yourself, "I can have that, too."

Stories are powerful. My cousin and I once told a story when we were little girls about how we were actually sisters and when we grew up, we would marry brothers. It was just a silly story we created when we were playing, but we began to tell it often. We told it to everyone and it made us smile. We didn't try to make it happen; we just enjoyed telling the story of it. Then, we let go of the story and went on to enjoy other things. Years later, we married brothers. It seemed like such a strange turn of events, but I now use it as a template when I want to create something in my life. I tell a story I enjoy and have fun telling it. Then, I let go of it and live my life.

We certainly didn't worry about how to make it happen, as young girls. By the time we were adults, if we even thought about the story, we would smile at how fun it was to think that way, but it wasn't as important to us now that we had grown up. We just both wanted to find a future spouse and didn't care who their brothers were. The fact that we weren't holding on tightly to making it happen, and that we had so much fun telling the make-believe story when we were younger, were the two elements that attracted the brothers. Remember, when you want to create something, tell the story lightly and joyously. It should be fun to do. Then, forget it and go live. You may be surprised when it shows back up in your life.

My Circumstance is Special

If you are telling yourself that it's going to be harder to find a mate because you are gay, transgendered, disabled, divorced, or have other challenges, this too is just a story. Stop buying into it. There are many happy gay couples. There are many happily married people with disabilities. There are many people who find fabulous relationships after one or more divorces. There are many transgendered people who have incredible relationships. There are many who don't want to get married, who easily find people who want the same kind of relationship. It doesn't matter who you are or what type of relationship you want to have, you can create it.

Sean Stephenson is a great example. He was born with osteogenesis imperfecta, stands just three feet tall, has fragile bones, and must use a wheelchair. He also married a beautiful woman, has a lucrative coaching career, has written best-selling books, and has a set of six-pack abs. He didn't let other people's beliefs about what someone with his health condition could accomplish. He embraced positivity and now has a fabulous life and a happy relationship. You can, too.

If you are worried about what other people think about your relationships, stop. That social worry keeps you from creating the relationships you want. There are other people out there who would be perfect for you. You find them by shifting your beliefs about relationships and raising your vibration to match the type of person you want.

Be Yourself

You are worthy of a relationship, just as you are. If making changes will make you happier, then make them. But don't change yourself to make someone else happy. If you do attract a relationship from that space, it won't be a happy and fulfilling relationship. If you want to lose weight or try something new, do it for you first. Changing any aspect of yourself simply to make someone else happy never works. You can't continue to pretend to be something you are not long term. It drains your energy and saps your joy. You are sending yourself a message that you are not good enough as you are to have a relationship and that will lower your vibration around the subject of romantic relationships.

No one sets out to create a relationship which makes them feel like they need to change to be loved, so if that starts happening, you are either in the wrong relationship or you just need to relax and let your partner love you as you are. If you see this as a pattern happening within your relationships, it almost always means you need to work on loving yourself as you are. "Like attracts like" so if you love yourself as you are, then you will attract others who will too. If you don't love yourself, you will never be able to change enough to suit someone else, and it will be an ongoing dynamic. The more you change, the more you will feel you need to continue to change to please your partner. Love yourself as you are right now, and allow your partner to do the same.

There are over seven billion people on this planet. It's fiction that there's only one out there for each of us. I'm thinking at least ten thousand, probably more, of them could be perfect for you—and would love you just as you are. You only have to connect with one of them.

How do you connect with a person who will love you for you? Be you! That's really all you have to do, along with focusing on your own vibration and being open to meeting someone.

I'm very spiritual and artistic. My husband is grounded and great at constructing material things. We are very different. If I had tried to be like him to attract him, not only would I have failed, I would have found misery. If we pretend to be someone we aren't, trust is eventually broken when you reveal who you really are. Not only that, it's too exhausting for anyone to continue to be someone they aren't. If you try, you will end up giving up not only your peace and happiness; your health will likely suffer, too. Truly, I don't think we can hide who we really are any more than an elephant can hide behind a fence post. We might think we can, but others can see through it.

Be Your Own Love

When you are looking for a new love, you might feel like you are missing something. The truth is, often we have to do or be what we think we seek from someone else, before someone else comes along who can give it to us. If you are waiting for someone else to make you feel loved, then it's likely that even if you find a wonderful partner, nothing they can do will make you feel loved for very long. If we are hoping for outside validation that we are lovable, we are bound to be disappointed. We need to know that we are lovable and love ourselves first.

Self-love improves every facet of your life. The more you care for yourself, the better your life will be. Self-love is not selfish. You have to raise your own vibration to be able to have energy to devote to others, and to be sustainably happy. Put your own life vest on first, or oxygen mask, as the travel metaphor may be. There are many ways to improve self-love, and I share some general self-love resources at the end of the book. For now, let's focus on ways to improve self-love that focus on romance.

We want to feel loved, adored, and secure in our romantic relationships. Think of how you will feel when you are in your ideal relationship and create ways to feel that way now. Some methods will be specific to you, but I'll share some examples of techniques you might want to try.

If you haven't read *The Five Love Languages* by Gary Chapman, you might want to look at it. He lets us know that different people can have different things that make them feel loved in a relationship. The five types he lists are: words of affirmation, receiving gifts, quality time, acts of service, and physical touch. Take some time to think of which of these appeal to you most, and then do things for yourself that satisfy those needs. Once you fill up your own love tank, you aren't so desperate for someone else to do it for you—and that makes you more attractive to others. This is also a great skill to use once you are in a relationship. You can use this to learn how to give to your partner and how to make requests from them. Remember, one person can't be everything to another, and you should still continue to give love to yourself. Love is a verb first, taking loving actions leads to loving feelings. Here are some ideas in each category:

Words Of Affirmation: Take the time several times a day to talk to yourself as you would a lover. Tell yourself how great you look, and how you appreciate the time you spent to style your hair or exercise and make your body feel great. It's helpful to look in the mirror when you do this. You can say these words in your head or out loud if you feel comfortable. Write yourself a love note, listing all the qualities you love about yourself.

I did this once and hid the letter—and I smiled so much when I found it years later. You might also want to leave little uplifting sticky notes around for you to see with messages like "You look awesome today." or "Thanks for being you."

Receiving Gifts: Buy yourself little things you enjoy. Don't hesitate to buy yourself flowers, jewelry, or other things that you would think of as a desirable gift from a significant other. You might want to sign up for a program like birchbox.com or graze.com that sends you samples of grooming products, healthy snacks, or something else you enjoy once a month in the mail. It will be like getting a surprise box of presents. You could also find a friend to exchange little gifts with once a month, if you like to be surprised.

Quality Time: Many of us feel strange about spending quality time with ourselves but it can be very rewarding. You can make dates with yourself to go the movies, lunch, hiking, etc. If you are a person who particular enjoys going on outings with other people then make plans to do these activities with your friends, and don't skip them even if you don't have a "date." I still recommend everyone taking time to have a "date" even for just an hour or two by yourself once a week; even once you have a romantic relationship. It can be transformative, helping you get more in touch with who you are and what you enjoy, when you plan an outing that no one has to enjoy but you.

Act of Service: You can take time to do things for yourself, too, which can sometimes be rewarding, like taking the time to cook yourself a special meal or organize a closet that has been bugging you. However, acts of service often make us smile because they represent a break from doing something we don't like to do. For example, my husband always drives when we go places together, because he knows I don't enjoy driving. Driving myself places wouldn't feel like an act of love, because I'm doing something I don't enjoy. Still, I could take a cab, bus, or even pay someone to drive me somewhere I need to go. You can pay someone to cook you a meal, clean your garage, or cut your grass. A nice way to say "I love you" to yourself is to pay someone else to complete something you dislike doing. If you are on a budget, look for a friend to swap tasks with. You could mow their lawn and they could clean your closet. Do things for each other that the other dislikes doing.

Physical Touch: This might seem like a tricky form of love to give yourself, but there are lots of ways to receive the sensory input "high touch" people crave. If you like massages, schedule them regularly and think of them as part of your self-care, not a luxury but a necessity. Also, take time to regularly caress your body with lotions that feel and smell good. Choose clothing and bed sheets that feel good on your skin. You can give yourself hugs and you can learn simple forms of healing touch, like Reiki, and do self-healing sessions. If you have a child you're close to, they love to give hugs and cuddles. Another way to help reach your touch quotient is to get a pet that likes to cuddle. I've had both cats and dogs that liked to sleep snuggled up to me or sit in my lap.

You can also fulfill your desire for touch in a way that helps others. I volunteered for a few years in a hospital, to rock and cuddle the premature babies. Often, these babies were in the hospital so long that their parents had to go back to work and the hospital staff didn't have time to just sit and hold them. These babies desperately need sensory input and caring for them will give you a smile that will last for days. I also have a friend who is known for giving hugs. He hugs everybody every time he sees them. He jokes that he just needs his daily hug quota, but I know he raises my spirit with his hugs. It's a way to be uplifting to others. You may want to find a community of people who like being "touchy," for example, Unity Churches are notoriously places where most everyone will hug you. One that I attended even had a part of every service where everyone went around and hugged everyone else. Even though I'm not usually hands-on with everyone, I admit this "hug therapy" was nice.

Making a List of Ideal Mate Qualities

Many law of attraction experts advocate making a list of qualities you want in a new romantic partner. I did this, but I don't think it's what brought me my love. In fact, while my husband does have many of the important qualities on that list, there are many he doesn't have— and now, I'm glad he doesn't. If it feels good to you to make a list, go for it. I might suggest that you try making a list of how your new love will make you feel instead of (or along with) lists of qualities you desire.

Also, when I feel the need to make a list, I always add the phrase, "this or something better," because I've learned that sometimes the universe knows more than me. Also, don't think that the universe is ever out to get you. Once, someone told me that she found a great guy who was everything on her list, but she forgot to write faithful on her list. Even though he was everything else she asked for, he cheated on her. She took to saying, "The universe has a nasty sense of humor." I would disagree. I think the universe and God want only the best for us—but they can only give us what we are vibrating. Take the time to feel how you want your relationship to feel. If lists or picture boards or telling the story gets you there, then that's the prompt to use. The tools and techniques are to get you to have (and learn to vibrate) the feeling you want to have.

How to be more attractive

In the last section, I told you to be who you are. Now I'm suggesting there's a way to be more attractive. It may seem contradictory, but it's not. I want you to be more attractive by being more of who you are, not less—and not turning yourself into something different altogether. You don't need any special grooming rituals, trendy haircut, or special perfume to be more attractive. You need to glow. You need to let your inner light shine so brightly that everyone who sees you can see it on your face.

I'll admit, this is something I've worked on for quite a while and I'm not quite there yet. Still, I met my husband before I was there, but I think the fact that I was working towards it was what made me more attractive. We all attract things that match us, so if we want to attract better partners, we want to raise our vibration, and improve our personal and relationship alchemy. That is not the same as becoming a different person. This is personal alchemy. It is a process of transforming by releasing the beliefs and thought patterns that are not really you—and getting closer and closer to your true essence. The closer you are to your true essence, the more you glow.

Look at people like Gandhi, Byron Katie, Martin Luther King Jr., and Mother Teresa. In terms of appearance, they glow because of the high level of vibration they have achieved. I find that more people seem to glow the closer they are to their true selves. Jesus, saints, and angels are depicted in art and illustration with a halo of light around their heads. It's the glow from being fully in their true essence. I believe we are created from love and, at our core, we are love.

Often, people in a new relationship and pregnant women are said to glow. Both are examples of people engaged in the joy of creating something new. We can learn to extend that joy and that connectedness to our true selves, so that we always glow. One thing I have noticed about people who glow is that they are always beautiful, no matter what their facial features or body type. The glow of love overshadows all that.

How do you increase your glow?

- *Do things you love.* When you take time to do activities that bring you joy, you will glow more. You will also feel passion. Since feeling the feelings you want in a relationship helps bring one to you, passion is very good for relationship creation.

- *Help others.* When you act in a way to help others, it takes the focus off you and it also brings you joy and makes you glow. It could also be a great way to meet new people—possibly the new partner you are looking for.

- *Be OK with who you are.* Dress in clothes that make you feel good. Style your hair in a way you love. Walk through the world with confidence. Send out loving vibrations to everyone you meet. You matter and you are more than worthwhile.

Exercises

Creating Your "Here and Now" Relationship

This is the exercise I shared with you in the beginning of the book. It's very simple to do. The only trick is to really get into the feeling of it. Create a fantasy relationship with just enough details to make it feel juicy. Don't get too caught up in how the person looks, or what their name is, unless it helps you feel it more fully. Play with it until you can feel the love flow when you think about your "lover." Then, make up the story about why they have to go—and why you are so happy because it is a wonderful thing for them and for your future. That even though you can't contact them while they are away, and you don't know exactly when they will be back, you know it will be wonderful once they return. You have promised them to thoroughly enjoy life while they are away and you plan to do so.

Every morning when you wake up, send him or her your love and think about the good times you've had—and the good times you will have once he or she has returned. When you go about your day, do it with the confidence and joy of a person who is deeply in love. Walk, talk, eat, and work in the energy of a person in the best relationship they could imagine.

Don't rush your love. Know that it's coming. Relax and enjoy this time to do whatever pleases you. You know you'll enjoy being reunited with your love, but you will be glad you also took the time to really enjoy and soak up your time being single.

If you find yourself getting disappointed that your relationship hasn't appeared yet, don't be hard on yourself. Be sweet. Go and do some of the items for yourself that make you feel loved. If you are sad, allow your feelings. Talk to a friend. Cry. It's okay. When you feel better, you can pick the story up again. Any technique we use here is to shift our vibration. We know that our vibration is rising when we feel good. If you find an exercise doesn't make you feel good, then stop doing it. Sometimes we just need to rest, allow, and be.

Sending Out Love Beacons

Are you sure you are ready for a relationship? If you believe you are, but it hasn't happened yet, make a formal intention. Write it down and put it in a safe place. You can write out the reasons why you want a new relationship and commit to keeping your heart open for it. Here is an example:

> "I have opened my heart for a new relationship. I am committing myself to a relationship that will create joy and contentment in both myself and my new love, and increase the love vibration of all we come into contact with."

Once you feel your intention in place, try this visualization. You can do it as often as it feels good.

Close your eyes and relax. Take a few deep breaths. Picture your heart—and feel with your soul—to discern if there are any walls built up around it. If you feel only walls, visualize knocking them away. Allow the bricks to be made of foam, so they are easy to remove.

Once any obstacles to your heart are gone, picture your heart opening. For me, that feels like petals of a flower are opening in my heart. You could also visualize your heart growing in size or surrounded by pulsating white light.

Once you feel that your heart is as open as it could be, picture the words "New Love" written on your heart. Feel the vibration of your heart with a new love and then picture little beacons of your love vibration going out into the world, seeking people who are a match to you.

Ask them to find the person who is the current best match for you and to guide you both toward each other by the strands of energy attached to the love beacon you send out. Ask that you will know each other when you find them. Then, sit and feel the love vibration as long as you wish.

BONUS!

Sign up and receive your free audio:

- How I Almost Instantly Manifested a Man

dailyalchemy.com/relationship-alchemy

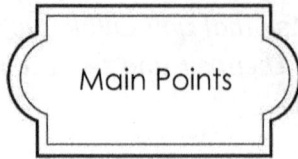

Main Points

- You are worthy of a great relationship.

- Drop any negative stories you have about relationships. You may have to look under the surface of your thoughts and stories to find some hidden ones. Others are drawn to you and your work based on the vibrations associated with you and your work.

- Tell stories about relationships that make you smile and then release them. Meanwhile, go out and live life to the happiest you can imagine.

- It doesn't matter what kind of relationship you want, you can create it.

- The person you want to attract will love the real you. Don't try to change who you are to attract a relationship. Shine your own light and find your own glow.

- Be your own love by giving yourself the kinds of love you are dreaming of receiving from a new partner; allow your feelings and be kind to yourself.

Chapter Five:

Using Alchemy to Improve Your Romantic Relationships

IMPORTANT: If your romantic partner is threatening, abusive, mean, or makes you feel bad about yourself, please SKIP this chapter. Go on to the next chapter, and focus on creating an easy breakup.

Am I saying that you can't manifest a new, improved version of them in your life? No, sometimes people even manifest lottery wins—but most of them don't end up happy in the long run. It's not worth the energy it would require, especially when the stakes are so high. Don't spend your time and energy trying to change someone who behaves badly, if you have a choice. You always have choice in your romantic relationships. Again, there are over 7 billion people on the planet, so work on your personal alchemy and you'll attract one that treats you right.

Many years back, my husband and I had reached a rough patch in our lives. I had just given birth to our fourth child. She was an unplanned blessing. We had planned for two children, but our second pregnancy produced twins and then fifteen months later, we had our last little miracle. We had recently moved over eight hours away from any family and friends, and were starting over in many ways, including opening a new business. Money was tight and we had 4 children ages six and under, three in diapers. We fell into our bed exhausted at night, but one of the little joys I could count on was cuddling with my husband while we slept.

One night, my husband turned away and didn't want me near. Night after night, he kept to his side of the bed. He no longer snuggled up to me or held my hand as we fell asleep. I felt alone. We didn't really have time to connect during the day and we were exhausted from getting the new business off the ground and taking care of the children. It was easier for me to stay relaxed through everything because I had my spiritual practice and meditation to ground me, but his behavior began to worry me. If he left, how would I care for 4 young children by myself?

I knew laying there, worried that he was unhappy and wanted to leave us, would not make things better. Yet, he didn't want to talk about what was troubling him. The more I pushed him, the more he pulled away. Unconsciously, I was being sucked into his unhappiness, and in turn focusing my thoughts and my energy on the wrong things. I wasn't following my own spiritual beliefs. Instead, I was getting sucked into a downward spiral of worry.

I decided to imagine everything was fine, and chose to act as if it was already true. Even if he left, everything would work out. I started focusing my own thoughts and energy on being happy again. I relaxed about our business, and I enjoyed spending time with the children. Happiness became my number one priority again. At night, when he kept to his side of the bed, I imagined that I was snuggled up to him, feeling loved and adored. Weeks passed with him staying distant— yet I was sleeping contently, feeling that I was somehow cared for. Then, one night, my husband snuggled up to me again. He began to smile more and get happy again. Once I held the vibration of happiness, he was able to reach for it, too. I had to be OK either way, though. Everything in our lives shifted, and got better after we got happy again.

Everything is Wonderful—and It Keeps Getting Better

Even when our romantic relationships are going well, we can start to create drama. Humans crave new expansion, and many of us have not learned how to make life exciting without creating drama. We might hold a belief that life has to have ups and downs and that we can't be happy all the time. We can create a different belief, that our relationship is wonderful, and even that it keeps getting more wonderful. It will naturally get better and better over time, if we line up with that vibration. We can set that intention for ourselves and our relationships, and be aware that we need to create new experiences which are positive. Then, we are able to stir up some energy in a more positive way. Here are some ways to create more fun and love in your relationship:

Create a statement of being for your relationship: In my first book, *Personal Alchemy*, I advocate creating a personal statement of being. Since your relationship has its own energetic entity, you can come up with its own statement of being. Here are the steps to create a personal statement of being, which can be easily modified for relationships.

My current personal statement of being is:

> I am a radiant, beautiful, magical author, alchemist and teacher who expands the joy, love, magic, and delight in my life and the lives of those I touch.

Here are a few simple steps to creating your own statement of being:

• Start with the words "I am," then list the traits and roles which best reflect who you have decided to be in the world. Then add the word "who" and fill in what you are going to do in the world.

• Think big. You are already impacting the world every single day. You might as well decide how you want to do it.

• Once you get it written in a way that makes you smile, memorize it. Also, write it down in places you will later see it.

• Follow your decisions and be who you have decided to be. No one can stop you.

• Don't share this with anyone, unless you are 100% sure they will be supportive.

My marriage's relationship statement of being is:

We are fun-loving, healthy, joyous, business owners, parents, and deeply connected souls who live full out, travel, bond with our family and friends, and delight in giving and receiving joy in the world.

The steps for making a statement of being for a relationship are pretty much the same as for making a personal statement of being, but instead you will start with the words "we are" instead of "I am" and you will focus on your relationship's goal in the world. Even if that goal is simply to support both of you in your happiness, that is enough. Two more happy people can help raise the vibration of the whole planet and inspire others to create happy relationships as well. If you have a relationship in which you feel comfortable in creating a statement of being together, it can be a wonderful bonding project. If not, you can craft it yourself and keep it your secret. It doesn't diminish its power. You can also make these statements for families, friendships, and businesses.

Shared Love Lists: Create lists of activities that make you feel loved by the other person. Some examples could be: make me a cup of coffee, write me a love note, rub my shoulders, sing to me, put gas in the car, etc. Then exchange lists and commit to doing one or more items for each other from the list every day. I have found that loving actions often create loving feelings and doing things for my husband makes me feel more connected to him.

Receiving loving actions from that person is wonderful, too. This works best when you can each make lists for the other to choose from, but if you have a significant other who is resistant to this, you could come up with a list of items you believe they would like and do those for them consistently.

A lot of times this happens very naturally in a relationship, but it's nice to put the added intention on small acts of service to be an expression of love that will raise the relationship's vibration. Intention makes the outcome stronger. I make my husband coffee and bring it to him most mornings, because he likes to have coffee before he gets out of bed. My husband always drives everywhere we go, because he knows I don't like to drive. We didn't plan those exchanges from a list at first, but as we've learned about loving actions with intention, these little acts take on much more significance.

Don't make it a competition of who does more for each other, but if you have a relationship that feels very one sided, you might need to address that differently. It is good to each make a list of items which make you feel loved if you can, to avoid misunderstanding. Your partner might be doing something they think is loving, such as doing all the grocery shopping so you don't have to. If that's not something you recognize as an act of love, it creates discord in the energy. They believe they are doing loving acts, and can't understand why you, their partner, are acting like you are not receiving love.

Start a New Hobby as Couple: Try something new that interests both of you. Take up sailing, painting, cooking, really any hobby or activity that adds new energy to the relationship, and that you both are interested in doing together. You could also start a new project, such as starting a business or writing a book together. My husband and I work together at a business we created, and we spent many hours bonding with each other as we built our business. Many people tell us that they couldn't stand to work with their spouse, and they need that time away, but it works for us. We have different hobbies that we do without each other, but working together is fun for us. Every relationship is unique, and what draws one couple together might not work for you. Make sure you choose to do activities together that you both sincerely want to do. Don't pretend to be interested for your partner's sake. That won't achieve the vibration that you want.

Spend time apart: Balance time apart with time together. My cousin and his wife love to travel and participate in outdoor adventures. However, he is afraid to fly, while she is not. Every year, they plan and make one or two trips together and one or two trips apart. It works out perfectly for them. They each get to do what they love, and neither is pressured to do what they don't enjoy. She likes tropical locales and travels there without him. He likes colder climates, and being away from civilization, so he does those trips alone. Together, they camp, hike and bike in places they both want to see and experience. When you do things separately, you both bring new energy back into the relationship. Just because you love each other, does not mean that you will love all of the same things. When you engage in activities you are passionate about, you bring the vibration of passion back to your relationship. Plan it out with your partner in a way that works for both of you. Decide if you want to take separate trips, or if you just prefer to have a certain number of days per week or month to engage in your own activities. If you haven't tried this in the past, and you are afraid your partner won't agree to it, tell the story of how they think it is a fabulous idea. If both partners aren't secure enough to do separate activities sometimes, then consider that some healing is needed in the relationship.

Couples' Bucket Lists: Create a list of things you would love to do together, without regard to whether or not you believe you can afford them, have the time or knowledge to do them, or other constraints. Choose one to do first, and then do it! Even if it takes several months or years to plan or save money for it, commit to the action. Consider deciding to do 10 or so items on your list every year. Some might be relatively easy, such as going zip-lining, while others, like a trip to Europe, may require more time, planning, and resources. Maintain your own lists for activities that your partner isn't interested in doing, and commit to those during your alone time.

Plateaus are Natural

Plateaus are natural occurrences. Whether you are working on learning something new, losing weight, or growing a business, there are periods of time where you feel like you are putting in the same level of effort or more—and nothing new is happening. You may also feel this in your romantic relationships over time. You are used to one another, engaging in the same routines and are starting to feel bored or stuck.

Don't take a plateau as a bad thing. If your relationship doesn't feel like it's getting better or worse, it is just catching up with your vibration. Tell the story about how this is perfect for you, for right now.

Maybe it's time for you to work on each of your personal goals for a while and then come back to work on your combined goals with new energy and strength. I've often heard that when something you are creating takes longer to get here, it means it's going to be even better than you expected. I like that story because it's positive, so I tell it when manifestations are slow. Plateaus are the same way. They are a time period where vibrations are building up to and will boost you to a magical new level. Relax, just keep adding to the positive energy, and you'll pass the plateau in no time. Once you do, your relationship will be stronger and more joyful.

What about sex?

Sex is one of the reasons many of us want a romantic relationship. It can be a deep form of intimacy, though hopefully not the only one in our romantic relationships. If we don't feel emotionally intimate, then sex can lack feeling and become more of just an empty act. I'm writing from the feminine perspective, but I think most everyone truly wants a deep connection from sex. Most people who engage in casual sex eventually find it lacking without a deeper connection.

If your sex life doesn't fulfill the desires you have for it, first look at your relationship alchemy. How do you feel about your relationship apart from sex? How do you get along and connect with each other? If your relationship doesn't feel deep and connected in other areas, you might want to focus on your relationship alchemy as a whole first and see if that is enough to shift your sex life.

If your relationship is great apart from sex, but your physical relationship is not satisfying, then you might have some beliefs about sex itself that could benefit from changing. Do you know what you want from sex? Don't be afraid to do some research or try new things. Many people learn about sex from porn, but there are lots of spiritual sexual practices, such as tantra, and other outlets for non-pornographic sexual lessons, such as www.pleasuremechanics.com.

First decide what you want, or do some research and investigation with your partner. We have the internet and you can find all kinds of information with a simple Google search. Sex is like anything else we desire. Feeling bad about it can only bring negative results, so tell the empowering story of how sex is a joyous, intimate, delicious part of your life—and it will be. Tell the story of your sex life how you want it to be. If you were raised in an environment that made sex "bad" or withheld information, you can get the information and perspectives you need now, as an adult.

Many people have personal histories that include inappropriate or unwanted sexual contact. I'm not condoning what anyone else did to you, but don't let the past event steal your present sex life. I'm not a fan of focusing on what is wrong. There are many forms of therapy that are healing, but when we just talk over and over about the events and people that hurt us in the past, it can keep us stuck there. It can also become an excuse to justify our own inaction, because we are afraid of going after what we want. If you have experienced this situation, you can heal it. Go back in the past and imagine the situation resolved differently. Imagine it not happening at all. That person didn't come into your life or instead, you went out of town the summer it took place. This story crafting is not to let them off the hook for what they did. It's to let you off the hook and move forward without those old stories.

Also, memories aren't permanent. They evolve into memories of memories, and scientific research is now demonstrating that memories can be changed. Psychologist Elizabeth Loftus, then of the University of Washington, proved how easy it is to implant a false memory when she 'tricked' adults to remember childhood events that didn't happen. Other researchers found that identical twins will often have different memories about events they both experienced and both will recall that they were the one who fell off their bike in the historic account.

The key here is that memories are changeable, so you can intentionally take the time to write out or visualize a different version and train your brain to believe a new version of events that is not so painful. In fact, you may have made it more painful and debilitating than it needed to be.

I once read about a man whose back was injured when he fell off a swing as a child and he had back pain and difficulties ever since. He did a visualization where he imagined the day that he fell, and in the new version, he either chose not to swing that day or hopped off before he fell. After doing this exercise, he no longer had any back pain or problems. Whether or not visualizing a different past works for you to that degree, if you have a bad historical experience, sexual or otherwise, this can be healing. You can heal any experience that hurt you, from molestation as a child to a painful comment from a past lover.

I do not mean to make light of our pain, but if it's in our past, we can choose to let it go. I had some negative sexual experiences myself, but they don't affect me anymore. The strange part is that after doing this process, I can remember feeling upset about negative occurrences, but I don't have any connection to those bad feelings anymore. It's like watching someone else's movie where I have no direct emotional investment. You might decide that you want to hold onto your pain for now and that's your choice. You can always decide to let it go later.

If it was my partner who had these difficulties, I would work on it by sending white light and healing thoughts to him. I would not think of him as broken or damaged and I would do everything I could to make him feel safe, comfortable, loved, and nurtured in our relationship. Practice seeing yourself as a strong, sexually desirable person, who is focused on healing and creating the best stories about your own sex life that you can. Have fun. Sex should be an enjoyable part of life.

Breaches of Trust

From an alchemy and law of attraction perspective, the most important part of any breach of trust is how you feel about it. If you or your partner cheated or lied to one another, it may feel like that relationship is beyond repair. That is not necessarily so. Take some time to sit down and feel your vibration and then feel the vibrations of the relationship.

Make a decision, based on how you feel about the relationship alchemy or how it feels vibrationally, as to whether it will benefit you to stay in the relationship. If it feels this is a symptom of a problem that you don't want to work to heal, it's best to start focusing on an easy breakup. If it feels like this relationship energy is positive and you desire to heal it, whether you were the person who caused the breach or not, begin to heal it. Begin to feel the rise in the vibration of the relationship, tell the story of how it was healed and talk in those terms when you talk about the breach with your partner. If they do not want to heal the relationship and want to separate, I would suggest focusing on the emotional work of letting the relationship go.

One of two things will happen: once you let go, they may decide they want to heal the relationship, too, now that they aren't feeling resistance or pressure from you; or you get to take time to heal yourself and begin a new relationship. I know, I know... I might as well have told you to create a nuclear reactor out of spare parts in your garage. Letting go of a relationship is not something many of us have an easy time doing, so if that's where you are, flip to the next chapter and we'll take that on at a deeper level. Just know, no matter what, you will be OK. Life will get better.

Help Out of a Downward Spiral

Lola Jones, the creator of Divine Openings, says we never actually stand still, we're either traveling in an upward spiral or a downward spiral. If you feel like your relationship or your feelings about it are on a downward spiral, you need to shift your thoughts. Jon Robinson, in the book, *Communication Miracles for Couples*, describes an activity designed to stop arguments in their tracks. He suggests couples who are arguing stop immediately, lie down (if possible), spoon each other, and breathe in sync for five minutes. He finds that if both partners will agree to do this, most fights quickly dissolve from this simple act of love and seeking alignment with each other.

I think this is a great, practical approach to quickly turning around a situation that is spiraling out of control. I also think, as a daily practice, it can help both halves of a couple to get and stay in vibrational alignment with each other. Intentionally creating that alignment (before fighting begins) is a great way to heal and/or strengthen a romantic relationship. See "Daily Love Sync" below for more details.

Exercises

Daily Love Sync

Create a ritual with your love that bonds you together and raises the vibration of your relationship. There are so many fun ways to do this and I think many people create them unconsciously when they start their relationship, but they tend to fade away over time. Some ways couples do this is creating individual language, like code words or nicknames they share with each other. Some books recommend kissing for five seconds, every time, before you leave each other. Some couples might have a morning or evening ritual, or even both. I know one couple who simply holds hands while they sit and talk on their deck or at the breakfast table every morning.

We sync our electronic devices every day, and thereby get our information up to date, so we want to do that with each other in our relationship. You can create it any way you want to, but you probably want to include ways that meet both partners' connection needs.

My husband and I have different ways that we prefer to connect. I'm a very feeling person, so I need to feel his energy to connect. Before we leave each other we kiss, hug, give each other's hands a little squeeze or all three. We often hold hands in our sleep for much of the night. Our palms have chakras or energy centers in them, and when we hold hands, we can feel each other's energy. I think that is why people enjoy holding hands. Because my husband is more analytical, we also take time in the evenings to touch base on how our day was, on a scale of 1 to 10. We will let each other know if we need help to improve our moods, or if there are problems in our relationship causing a low vibration.

We don't talk in depth every night. Many days, it's just a check-in to confirm that all is well. I know some couples who tell each other three things they appreciate about each other every night before they go to bed. There is also a very simple tantric exercise that is usually referred to as the circle of light, in that both partners sit facing each other or close together with their legs entwined. They take turn gazing into each other's eyes for 3 or 4 minutes and sending love. Then the other partner takes a turn and you go back and forth sending and receiving for as long as you like. Sometimes even just stopping to take a moment to actually look deeply in each other's eyes at least once a day can be enough to help you connect.

We sync up in different ways because we are both different personalities who process and communicate information in different ways. I think of James Cameron's movie *Avatar* in which the Na'vi race would tell each other "I see you." They were talking about seeing each other's souls. We need to take time daily to "see" our significant other in a way that connects us and reminds us why we chose to be together. Take some time to come up with a way to sync up daily with your partner that suits your relationship. It's worth it.

Love Vibration Mixology

There are several vibration mixology techniques you can do on your own in my book, *Personal Alchemy*, and there is an eKit on my site that walks you through all kinds of them. I recently tried to actually do these with my partner and found it to be profound although only taking five to ten minutes. Do this when you have quiet time together and aren't in a rush to go anywhere. It could be done before going to bed in the evening or before making love. Here are the steps, feel free to modify to meet your needs.

- Sit facing your partner. First feel your own vibration. Take the time to get quiet and go through whatever steps you need to get in touch with your own inner being, feel where you are vibrating. Let your partner do the same. You can do this part with your eyes open or closed, whichever is easier for you, but rest your hands on your lap with palms up.

- Once you can feel your own vibration, hold your hands up, chest high, palms facing out toward your partner. Send your vibration out to them, while they send theirs to you. Lightly look into each other's eyes as you do this step.

- After a few minutes, clasp both hands and intents in order to mix the energies. Sit and just feel the sensations that come up as you do this step. When it feels complete, give each other a long, heart to heart hug.

I find this activity works best if done in silence, focusing on feeling each other's vibration and the alchemy of the relationship itself. It you don't think your partner would do this, you can do it alone—with their higher self—in visualization, but ask them first.

My husband is not nearly as spiritually oriented as I am, but I ask him to try things for me as part of my research, etc. I just make it light and say, "I know this might sound weird, but do you mind helping me out by...?" Sometimes he enjoys it, and sometimes he doesn't, but he usually is open to try it at least once. Tell the story of how your partner is open and receptive to trying new things.

BONUS!

Sign up and receive your free audio:

- Vibe Mixology for Love Relationships

dailyalchemy.com/relationship-alchemy

Main Points

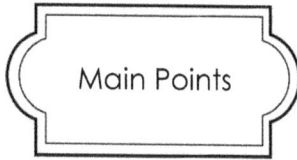

- Don't try to make a relationship better with someone who is abusive; manifest a smooth exit instead.

- Learn how to create positive drama in your relationships.

- Do new activities with your partner and by yourself so you can bring new energy back to your relationship to allow it to grow.

- Plateaus are natural and only represent a problem if you feel bad about them.

- You can heal past negative sexual memories.

- Sex is meant to be yummy, fun, connecting, and nurturing.

- Breaches of trust don't have to be the end of a relationship. Feel the vibration around them.

Chapter Six:

Using Alchemy To Create Boundaries & Exit Relationships

My Facebook page is my utopia. It's a place where I can express myself freely and connect with other wonderful people. If someone writes negative posts, I hide their feed. If someone writes negative responses to my posts, I will unfriend them and block, if necessary. For my business page, I give no second chances, anything ugly and you are immediately banned and blocked.

I don't have time to engage negativity, and social media is a place where I don't have to do so at all. One of my relatives liked to make "funny" comments about all of my posts on Facebook. I know he meant to be humorous and he is a very close relative, so I let it continue for a while. I told myself I needed to shift the way I thought about the posts, which was definitely an option. I worked on not letting his comments bother me. However, one day, a particular comment hit me hard and brought tears to my eyes. I knew that this was my problem, not his. He did not mean to hurt me, he meant to be humorous. Still, I unfriended him on Facebook, and I suddenly felt light and free. I noticed I had stopped posting things that made me happy because I was afraid he would ridicule me. I created a boundary around my Facebook page not to hurt the other person, but to create the safe space I desired.

Boundaries

In my extended family, we "do forgiveness" or at least act like we forgive, very well. After I learned that one of my uncles' wives ran away with another of my uncles, I was amazed that they all sat at the same holiday table, smiling at each other. My mother raised me with beliefs our family holds dear: other people's feelings are important, other people's comfort is a priority, and family is important. I still believe all of those things, but I've also decided to believe, in addition: my own feelings are important, I can be of service to others without sacrificing my own needs and wants, and I can love my family and create boundaries for interacting with them. You may not have any problems with creating healthy boundaries, but many people have beliefs that make them suffer in silence instead of setting up ground rules.

Look at how you feel about your own family and friends and the way you interact with them. Do you enjoy and savor get-togethers or do you dread them? Do you agree to go to events you'd rather not attend because you are afraid of hurting someone's feelings? Have you outgrown friendships, but continue them because you don't know how to end them?

See if you can make a list of your known and hidden beliefs about your relationships by looking at how you actually act. You may say that you save the weekends for your immediate family or your sweetie, but do you answer calls and texts all weekend or give in and go meet friends when you don't want to? There's no need to make a list of rules that you have to follow, but make sure you consciously decide how you want your relationships to work. Some people don't have cell phones, even though their family members really want them to carry them. It feels better, to them, not to have that energetic pull of a cell phone around. I also know several people who spend days in silence each month because it feeds their soul. I do this myself occasionally, when I have mornings that I'm alone. Some people don't like to have people come to their homes, but prefer to get together in restaurants, etc. It's your life! You make the rules!

Find out which kinds of interaction raise your vibration. It will be specific to you. You might thrive on a house full of company and love cooking for them, or you might find that overnight visitors drain your energy. Politely inform others what works for you and what doesn't. If you don't like having houseguests and someone asks if they can come, just let them know that having someone spend the night is not convenient. Let them know you can find a local hotel for them and you can plan out time you can spend together while they are in town.

Some people will not like the boundaries that you implement. My relative was not happy to be unfriended on Facebook and I had to deal with the repercussions. I explained to him that while I knew he was attempting to be humorous, his comments hurt me. Further, I felt if I cut out that interaction, then I would not get hurt by a comment that was not even meant to hurt me. He still wasn't happy about it, but that's okay. Our job isn't to make everyone else happy. It's to make ourselves happy, and to provide an example for others. Does that mean we should be unkind or not help others? No, I find that a lot of my happiness comes from giving to others.

However, I get to decide the ways in which I choose to care for others. I strive for the win/win situation when giving.

Introverts and extroverts

We all probably have characteristics of both, but most of us usually lean one way or the other. We either gain energy from being with other people or we gain energy from spending time alone. Neither way of being is better or worse than the other. We need both introverts and extroverts for the world to function. Our job is to know what level of alone time, and what level of social time, works best for us—and follow it.

If you need to be with people every day to raise your energy, find people to interact with. If you need to spend several hours alone each day, respect yourself enough to make that happen. Take the time to figure out what works for you and implement it thoughtfully.

Most of us don't want to be in a large group of people all the time or alone in a cave continuously either. Take the time to find what balance of interaction works for you. If you need time alone, put it on your calendar. When someone asks you to do something during "your" time, let them know you have an appointment and aren't available then. Appointments with yourself are just as important as appointments with other people. If you are someone who needs to be with other people, don't let others make you feel as though you socialize too much and need to be more inwardly focused. It's your life, so set the interpersonal and energetic boundaries to make it work for you.

When to Call it Quits

Sometimes, boundaries aren't enough. If people don't respect our boundaries and our vibrations lower because of our interactions with them, we can choose not to keep them in our lives. We all make mistakes and hurt each other and that in and of itself doesn't necessarily mean we need to separate. The problem comes when we feel like we need to determine if it's "right" for us to separate. We may try to gain other people's approval to continue or end a relationship. Other people don't know how the relationship feels from the inside. They do not know the alchemy of your relationship and how the people involved affect each other. Make your own decision from within, by tuning in to your own wisdom and your own vibrational energy.

Usually we know whether or not we should continue a relationship. If we feel torn, it's often not because we don't know the truth, but because we don't like the truth. The truth may be that we don't mix well with this person, but we are afraid to be without them. The truth may be that we are as much at fault as they are and we need to work at healing the relationship.

I like to remind myself that there are no mistakes. If I continue a relationship that should end, eventually it will become more and more uncomfortable until it ends. If I let go of a relationship that could have been saved, I will get to create that same energy with another person. It will all work out, and if you don't know what to do, let the relationship simmer and work on your own personal alchemy first. If you work on yourself and raise your own vibration, you in turn attract better relationships. You are an ingredient in all of your relationships and you greatly affect the outcome.

I love the story from Catherine Ponder about the boss who no one wanted to work for. One secretary was assigned to him and she treated him like he was a wonderful boss. Toward her, he behaved as one. No one in the office could believe how he had changed, until she left—and he went back to being impossible again. Here's the thing: people have free will, so the boss may have left—or asked for another secretary to be assigned— instead of being pleasing to work with for this particular high-vibration secretary. We all need to know that if we focus on our vibration and do what we need to do to be happy, people are either going to fall in line and get happy with us or leave our lives. We have to be OK either way.

The one caveat is that if someone is abusive toward us, it's hard for us to raise our own vibrations while allowing that to continue. We need to try to escape that first and then attract better relationships as we grow.

Create a Smooth Breakup

If you decide that you need to end a relationship, take a little bit of time to envision a smooth breakup. Remember that when one relationship ends, it gives both parties the opportunity to make new and perhaps better-suited connections.

Most of us don't want to hurt other people's feelings, so we avoid telling someone we don't want to spend time with them anymore. If it is a casual relationship, you may not really need to do much, but it is kind to tell a social friend that you have several new obligations and won't be available anymore. You may or may not feel it necessary to go deeper into it than that. If you know that their behavior causes them to lose other relationships, it might be beneficial. However, if you are in a very close or romantic relationship, you owe your partner an explanation. Don't just stop calling or avoid them. Let them know that the relationship isn't working. Take time to write out a scenario in which they are as content about the breakup as you are, and do this before you have the hard conversation. Let it be as easy as possible.

The only time not to tell someone you wish to break up is if you are in a situation where you fear for your safety. If you have any inkling that the person might be violent, then do what you need to in order to stay safe. Picture them not caring at all that the relationship has ended, and letting you go easily. Picture them being attracted to someone new. Do the exercises at the end of this chapter and keep yourself surrounded by white light, energetically cutting your own ties with them. Also, get help if you need it. Don't hesitate to go to a safe house or move, if the situation escalates and you no longer feel safe.

You can feel that person's energy, so if you don't feel safe, trust your intuition, and don't let anyone make you feel bad for doing so. We are all created from divine loving energy, but some people get so removed from that until they are expressing mostly darkness in their lives. Those people can be prayed for and sent light and love, but you deserve to feel safe and comfortable in the world. You will not be safe or comfortable if you let them continue to harass you.

Focus on being happy now. Sometimes, if we simply think we will be happy once we get someone out of our lives, or once we find the right person, we are stealing our own present happiness. Instead, we end up re-creating the same relationships over and over, because we are not growing. Whether you initiate a breakup, or someone else does, if you are ending a serious romantic relationship, take time to heal and focus on your happiness as a single person—before you dive back into dating.

Getting Over a Breakup

I read a wonderful blog written by a very spiritual guy all about enlightenment. He is incredibly wise and shares profound truths. A few weeks ago, his long-term girlfriend walked out on him and he became suicidal on Facebook and Twitter. All of his enlightened bliss went out the window and he shared his pain. He felt it full out. In a few short days, he was back to a place of bliss and excited about his new prospects for the future.

Some might think his behavior showed him not to be enlightened, but sharing his truth and being vulnerable helped him process his emotions fully and therefore quickly. In my experience, when we allow our emotions and feel them deeply, they heal quicker.

I don't subscribe to the plan that we should try not to be sad or angry when we are. I try not to share my emotions when they are still raw, but choose to feel them by myself and then discuss the issues once my own energy has shifted. We are human, though, and that doesn't always work. You know yourself and your own energy, but these are the rules I would make for myself for any major breakup:

1) Feel my feelings and be there for myself.

2) Reach out to friends or anyone to talk to if I need a listening ear.

3) Feel bad as long as I feel bad. There is no rule for how long you get to grieve.

4) Don't try to get the other person back. No matter how wonderful they are, there is someone more wonderful out there who will want to be with you. You deserve to be with someone who couldn't imagine not being in your life, and vice versa.

5) Take at least six months to a year off, to focus on loving yourself and taking care of yourself, before thinking about a new romance.

Exercises

Cutting Relationship Energy Cords

We are connected to every person that we have a relationship with by cords of energy. If we only meet someone briefly, it may be just light strands that fade away over time. People with whom we have long-term relationships or very intense relationships, are linked by stronger cords. Here are the steps I take to release energy connections:

1) Close your eyes and take a few minutes to center yourself and feel your own vibration. Get relaxed.

2) Think about the person you want to release. Get a picture of them in your mind. See yourself standing a few feet away. Look at the energy that links you. Is it a thick rope? It is a metal chain? Is it a crocheted string? What color is it? How does the energy linking you feel? Is it oppressive or does the connection feel good? How far does the energy stretch? Are you tightly bound to each other, or can you move freely?

3) Most likely, if this is a relationship you want to end, the energy bond does not feel good. Tell the person in the visualization, "I fully release you and set you free to find your own good. I am released as well and go to meet my good."

4) Take the cords that connect the two of you and pull them away from your body and visualize them dissolving. You can visualize poofing them away with a magic wand or cutting them with magic scissors. Visualize whatever works for you, but don't visualize them as though they are hard to break. Visualize them quickly disappearing with little effort.

5) Visualize sending love and light to the person you released and to yourself. Watch both of you

happily going off in separate directions, no longer energetically connected.

This is a good exercise to do if you want to end a relationship that you are afraid the other person won't want to end. You may need to do it a few times to check and make sure the energetic links aren't growing back.

Energetic boundaries: The Magic Bubble

Find a quiet place to sit or lie down. If you are out and about, you can even hide in a restroom. Close your eyes. Picture a beautiful, white light entering the top of your head, and slowly filling up your whole body. I call the white light God's love, but you could call it universal love or whatever sounds good to you. As this light fills up your body, imagine it relaxing you and taking away any stress you are feeling, replacing it with love. Once your whole body is filled with this white light of love, let it expand until it makes a bubble all around your body. Then, you can set an intention that no one can enter your bubble unless you wish them there, or that this love bubble will stay with you all night or day, depending on your desires.

I started doing this with my kids when they were little, to help them sleep or to use if they felt scared. I started using it myself when I was going somewhere I might feel uncomfortable. I learned, as I grew older, that a lot of what I thought was "social anxiety" was actually an ability to feel other people's feelings, which can be a good thing—but not when you don't want to feel them. I felt a lot of anxiety at sporting events, because I was picking up on everyone else's anxiety about the game. A lot of people have these empathic abilities, and many don't even realize it. If you find that sometimes you feel emotions, and you don't know why, this might be the cause.

Try taking the time to surround yourself with a bubble of love and intend to only feel your own feelings—and see what happens. It is also good when you know you are going to encounter a person, perhaps a relative or co-worker, who tends to push your buttons. You can put on your bubble of love and what they do won't bother you so much.

BONUS!

Sign up and receive your free audio:

- Cutting Relationship Cords
- The Magic Bubble

dailyalchemy.com/relationship-alchemy

Main Points

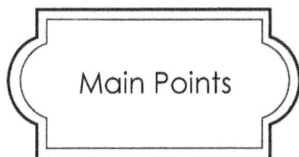

- Boundaries are necessary and there is no need to feel guilt about them.

- If boundaries aren't enough to make interaction possible, you can decide to cut ties with a person in your life.

- It doesn't matter if you are introverted or extroverted, as long as you honor your own needs.

- You can create a smooth breakup.

- If someone leaves you and it hurts, take the time to feel your feelings and heal.

Chapter 7:

Other Relationships & Situations

There are a few relationships that don't fit neatly into the other chapters, which can collectively make big impacts on our lives and can influence our personal and relationship alchemy. Here are a few of those relationship types that many of us encounter regularly.

The Two-Minute Relationship

We experience these on a daily basis. We come into contact with people for short periods of time: passing in an elevator, interacting with our waiter or waitress, standing in line at the post office, etc. We can choose such chance encounters and use them for growth, especially if we remember that no encounter is really by "chance." We are always attracting people into our lives who match our personal alchemy.

I have found that I often get to have the best clerks in a store and awesome wait staff when I eat in a restaurant. When I don't, instead of assuming that my vibration has lowered and I am attracting a less than ideal interaction, I assume that I am there to add some joy to their day. I always try to make people smile, or raise their spirits somehow, whenever I meet someone who seems to be having a tough day. Remember, happy people aren't mean or angry. You can't make someone be happy, but you can send them love and understanding—and that can make a huge difference.

I often share that I send out love and Reiki when I go on long car drives, standing in lines, or similar activities that can be frustrating. It does so much to increase and improve my own energy and I intend that it is helpful to those willing to receive it as well. I've learned that is important for me to remember to send out universal Love energy or Reiki energy, not my own energy.

When you let love flow through you to others, your own energy will increase. If you try to send out your own energy, you can find yourself depleted. Whether you send energy out to others, set an intention that every person you encounter will have a blessing for you and that you will have one for them. What you focus on, and expect to see, is what will happen.

Co-workers

Relationships with co-workers can be similar to relationships with family. We don't usually get to pick our co-workers and through work we often deal with a wide variety of people. Usually, some of those people become friends, and others may challenge us to grow. Often, you can deal with their behaviors in much the same way you do with family and friends, using whatever boundaries you are able to within the work structure.

While you can focus on raising your relationship alchemy with specific co-workers, it's good to also raise the vibration of your work environment itself:

1) **Create an Intention Vortex**: I do this first thing when I go into the office to work. My husband and I own a heating and cooling business, so it's not necessarily a spiritually-minded environment. I set the intention that our office is filled with love and attracts loving people. I picture the highest good for our employees and our customers. Our business runs very smoothly, with few problem customers and I believe my picturing this on a daily basis creates a vibration that attracts the best customers and employees.

   I do the same thing at my home. When you put love into a place over and over, it builds up into its own vortex of love. This is my favorite way to raise the vibration of a place, because you can do it anywhere without anyone else knowing unless you tell them. They'll probably feel it and maybe wonder why they feel so peaceful, but no one will disapprove or tell you to stop.

2) **Mini Feng Shui**: Feng Shui is a framework including a lot of different ways to direct the energy flow of buildings. It can be very complicated, but I prefer easy-peasy Feng Shui. I do two primary things to improve the energy of my work environment using Feng Shui. The first is to cut the clutter. If I don't love it and use it, it goes. This frees up so much energy.

It's easy to do, but if you'd like some guidance, I recommend the book *Clear Your Clutter With Feng Shui* by Karen Kingston. It's a simple to follow book that I pull out every year or so. Every time, I release more and more baggage and it feels so good! I deal with each piece of paper or e-mail as it arrives. I read it and immediately trash it or file it. Keep the energy clean in your workspace. It will improve all your work relationships, too.

The other Feng Shui technique I practice uses the Bagua, or the energy map. It is a square map which breaks buildings and rooms into sections of different areas of life. For example the right rear corner of a space is where to make enhancements to improve love and relationships, the middle is the space for health, etc. I look at the map and decide which vibration I want to increase. If it is the love vibration, I will choose something that stands for love in my mind (a piece of rose quartz, a statue of love birds, a picture of a heart, etc.) and place it in the love area of my office or on my desk. It can be out for others to see, such as a statue or picture or you can keep it private. I keep a picture of happy customers under my phone, which I put on the career section of my desk.

As with everything, the magic is in how much you enjoy it. So if you want to play with this, make it fun—not work. Your co-workers need not know it is anything other than simple desk decorations.

3) **Add a Pleasant Aroma**. I am partial to essential oils and I love my diffuser. You might like candles, incense, or fresh flowers. Everything has a vibration, and for that reason I like natural scents instead of synthetic ones, but if it makes you feel good—that's what counts the most. If you want to raise the vibration in a work environment where you have to keep sounds and smells low-key, you could keep flowers on your desk, or put a cotton ball with a drop of two of essential oil on it somewhere in or on your own desk. If even that is too much for your environment, just keep a bottle of your favorite oil (or other good smell) somewhere you can reach for it and take a quick whiff. Even a nice flavored lip balm could work.

Relationships with Animals

My dog, Lilly, is sitting here "talking" to me now as I write. She has become a treasured member of our family. Loving her is a blessing to us all. I find most animals tend to sense our feeling states and can help us process them. I had a cat who helped me heal when a long-term relationship of mine ended. He sat with me while I cried and I could feel the energy he sent me. He tended to me for months and although he was still there once I had healed, I knew that he was aware that I needed more energy from him when I was getting over the broken relationship.

Many animals are healers. If you find yourself going through a period of upheaval or change in your life, a pet could help you get through it. Animals have actually saved their owner's lives, but the number of people who have been emotionally saved by animals is innumerable.

Animals are also messengers. I've had many animals come into my life for a brief moment to send me a message. I love to look online or at the book, *Animal Speak: The Spiritual & Magical Powers of Creatures Great and Small* by Ted Andrews, for guidance about what an encounter with a certain animal might mean.

Awhile back, my family and I came across an injured great blue heron in our neighborhood that we tended to and took to the vet. I felt that the bird held a message for me. When I looked it up, the material regarding the great blue heron focused on people who were involved in many trades. I was going through a time when I had several pursuits, and I loved them all–and the bird gave me the message that it was right for me to continue to be involved in all the activities I loved, even if there were many.

Be aware of the animals around you. If you are looking for an answer to a question, they might have it for you.

Some people fear animals and there are times when we need to be cautious around certain animals. The best way to deal with an animal you fear is to feel for its vibration and send it love. Don't approach an animal you fear, but do send it love. If you have adopted an animal and it turns out you can't love and care for properly, don't feel guilty if you need to find it a new home. Like relationships with people, when we let go of an animal who is not a right fit for us, we allow them to find a home that is better for them. Set the intention to find the best home possible for them, and take the actions necessary to do so.

Animals play a huge role in the vibration of our planet. They bless us because they are always authentically themselves and not desiring to be someone else. There are many different ways to have connections with animals that will benefit you and the animal, so don't discount their role in your life.

In Jail or Otherwise Not Physically Free

I read Victor Frankl's book, *Man's Search for Meaning*, many years ago, but it is one of those rare books that changed me for life. Victor was a psychiatrist who survived the Nazi death camps during the Holocaust. His wife, parents, and brother died. From his family, only he and his sister survived. In his book, he shared his personal experiences, reflecting on the ways people reacted to their captivity and mistreatment and how their differing attitudes made a difference. The people who were the happiest were those who tried to help others, shared their meager food and spread joy and love in the worst of circumstances. As Frankl said, "The salvation of man is through love and in love."

I've never been in a situation where I was not physically free, although it may have felt that way at times when I was teenager. I can imagine it is one of the most difficult circumstances in which to focus on building relationship alchemy and giving love to others, but really what else is there to do? If you have been wrongly deprived of your freedom, as in kidnapped, obviously you will probably want to try to escape. Improving the relationship alchemy with those around you may actually make that easier. That is a rare occurrence, however—and it's more likely that people end up deprived of freedom because they are incarcerated through the commission of a crime.

Many people in jails have low vibrations and lack love for themselves. If you ever end up in this situation and have the self-awareness to work on raising your own vibration and those of the people around you, it could make a huge difference for the emotional well-being of everyone there.

Dr. Ihaleakala Hew Len worked with the worst prisoners in a Hawaiian prison, and he created an improvement in their behavior without ever seeing them. He did Ho'oponopono, an ancient Hawaiian practice of reconciliation and forgiveness, on their files, and in so doing sent them love and forgiveness. The most violent offenders changed their behavior, and needed less intervention to keep them under control. All he did was love the prisoners, and ask for their forgiveness on an energetic level, and they felt it and responded.

Hopefully, you will never end up in a situation where your freedom is taken from you, but if you do, remember our thoughts and feelings are still under our control. It is a wonderful thing to send healing energy to people who are somehow imprisoned. I have a friend who is a psychiatric nurse and works in a women's prison. She is a Reiki master and sends Reiki, a form of energy healing, to the prisoners and uses it when she treats them. The other employees don't know she does this but they always tell her that the facility is so much more peaceful when she is working. The connection she makes helps raise each prisoner's vibration and makes a difference. Before you think that prisoners don't deserve love, because they committed crimes to get there, consider that most of them suffer from a severe lack of self-love that may have contributed to their misdeeds. We are all worthy.

Relationships with the Deceased or Spirits, Angels

I still have a relationship with several people in my life who have passed on. I think when we have relationships with dead people and with any non-physical being, the important thing is to remember we are in a physical world and we need to live in it. We can connect with spirits, but in most cases the majority of our time should be spent focusing on the world around us.

That doesn't mean you can't communicate, receive messages, or assistance from non-physical beings. They can play a daily role in your life, just as long as they are helpers in your life and not the center of your life. I have received messages and assistance from deceased family members and angels alike. I invite them to participate in my life. I often connect with them during vivid dreams. My grandmother has come to soothe me during dreams, and other people who have passed have come to tell me they are OK in dreams.

Connecting with angels can be as easy as inviting them into your life. I learned from one of my favorite authors who writes about angels, Doreen Virtue, that I can invite in the angels of laughter, joy, peace, love, etc., based on my need. You can also learn about individual archangels and invite their assistance. Terri Lynn Taylor is another author who shared some great techniques for connecting with angels. Even if this isn't a subject you want to research more, you can connect with angels in your own way. You can set an intention to interact with angels and then watch for signs from them.

Exercises

Animal Connection Game

I like to play this game when I go to the zoo or take nature walks. I like to send out love and Reiki to any animals around and ask if they have a message for me. I have found that since I started doing this when we visit the zoo, almost all the animals will come right up to the edge and look at us. We never have problems seeing the animals and often they look me in the eye. Many of the animals in captivity need healing and love. I've also realized that many of them are content and enjoy interacting with the energy of the people who come to visit them. Luckily, most zoos are working to improve conditions for the animals there and you can feel how much better the energy is when this is done.

When I walk through nature and send out silent blessings to the animals, many of them come out to visit, too. Make your intention light and easy and don't be disappointed if you don't see any animals right away. If you pay attention, you may actually feel their energetic presence.

The Energetic Relationship Game

When we give someone something that we have touched or created, our energy signature is attached to it. If I receive a gift from someone, but have never met them, I still connect with their energy. I like to leave gifts for "random" people to find. I know that it will always find its way to the perfect person who aligns with the energy of the gift. Sometimes, I leave money in an envelope with a note saying it is a gift for the finder. My kids and I leave bottles of bubble solution and sidewalk chalk in the park with a note for children to find. We also place little uplifting notes tucked in our library books before we return them. There are so many fun ways to connect with people and uplift them without ever meeting them. If this sounds fun to you, these websites might inspire you: ripplekindness.org or www.1spark.net.

The second part of the game is to be open to receiving these "random" gifts yourself. I have been the recipient of many surprise treats from anonymous people. When I receive a free meal or an uplifting note, I try to feel the energy of the sender and flow love back to them.

BONUS!

Sign up and receive your free audio:

- Seeing the Beauty in Everyone

dailyalchemy.com/relationship-alchemy

Main Points

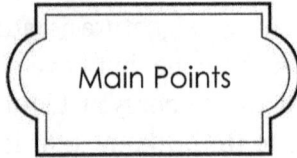

- Even people we interact with for a short period of time can have a profound impact on us.

- We can shift our relationship with co-workers by shifting the energy of our workplace.

- Animals are healers and messengers.

- Even while incarcerated, people can raise their relationship alchemy and help others.

- Our connections with deceased friends and family, along with angels, can benefit us and help us create higher vibrations.

Chapter Eight:

A Few Last Words on Relationship Alchemy

Relationships can be vehicles for growth, pathways to bliss, and tools to create more love on the entire planet. It's wonderful when relationships can fulfill multiple roles in our lives. The happier we are and the more we focus on raising our own vibrations, the happier our relationships will be. When we focus on the good in others and in our relationships, we indirectly raise our own personal vibration and, in turn, can create an upward spiral in which our own personal growth improves our relationships, which then deepens our personal growth and the whole of our lives begins to improve onward and upward. That's the way it was meant to be. Let your relationships be a source of joy and fun. Be thankful for every positive connection.

The reason I call Relationship Alchemy the "missing ingredient" to heal and create blissful family, friendship, and romantic relationships, is that techniques alone will not make relationships better. If your vibration is low when you think about or interact with a certain person, then all of the communication skills in the world won't help heal the relationship or change the dynamic between the two of you. People can feel how you feel about them, whether they feel it consciously or unconsciously, no matter how hard you may be trying to mask your negative feelings. I've experienced this with my own children. I followed the communication technique in a parenting manual exactly, but they didn't respond the way the book said they would. Did I do the technique wrong? Not necessarily, but techniques won't work for the long term if the energy behind them isn't sincere. If I was angry at the moment and just trying to get them to behave the way I wanted them to, they would be able to feel that and no technique would work. Relationship alchemy can make or break our relationships. Without positive vibrations in our relationships, they can seem fine on the surface, but it's all a facade that easily cracks when tested.

In contrast, is it true that if we have high relationship alchemy, we don't need to learn other relationship skills? Not necessarily. We aren't all born to be natural communicators. Many of us grew up in dysfunctional homes and didn't have great role models for how to interact with each other. Our parents may not have been the kind of people we want to pattern our love relationships to follow. Also, if men turned to porn to learn how to interact with women sexually, they could have learned some unhealthy patterns. I think learning communication skills, relationship care, and problem-solving techniques can be highly beneficial, especially once you have worked on your relationship alchemy.

Our relationships are like a swimming pool. Getting comfortable with water and feeling good about getting in, is the equivalent of what relationship alchemy helps us achieve. It's a very important part and it's enough for some people to know in order that they might stay afloat and enjoy the water. Once you have conquered that and you want to learn some creative or efficient ways to swim, studying techniques can be beneficial–even necessary, depending on your goals.

I've found several books, courses, and techniques that have helped me improve my relationships that I share as resources. You might want something that fits your specific situation. Tell the positive story that you will easily find all that you need, and then search online or in your neighborhood for some resources and see what appears.

Exercise

The 5-Minute Relationship Band-Aid

A moment of anger, sadness, or other negative emotion can arise anywhere. We might be at work, in a store, on the phone with a customer service provider—something challenging or mundane—and suddenly, we will feel our emotions bottoming out. If this happens, I recommend the following 3 steps:

1) *Feel the feeling.* Get to a place where you can be alone for a few minutes to feel your feelings without resistance or judgment. I usually excuse myself to the bathroom if possible. It's always a private space. Then I take a few minutes to feel the negative emotion in my body. I try not to think the thoughts that brought on the emotion, just feel the feeling as sensations in my body. If I can't be entirely by myself, I still try to calmly feel the feeling without speaking or reacting.

2) *Repeat a Mantra.* Once the feeling moves or I feel the energy shift in my body, I create a mantra to focus on the feelings I want to have instead. It can be, "this too shall pass," if I'm still upset, or "my husband treats me like gold," or even, "The cable company loves to give me fabulous service," if that is how I want to feel and what I want to experience. Think about the best thought you could think in this situation and make it into a mantra and repeat it.

3) *Take Inspired Action.* After a moment of repeating the mantra and a few deep breaths, do what feels right. You may choose to continue a discussion or you may try to find a tactful way to delay it until later. I'm not suggesting the inspired action is always an easy or a perfect solution. You can always call the cable company back later but you might not be able to reschedule a meeting with your co-workers. Remember, you're human, so if you don't handle a situation in a way that you wanted, forgive yourself, apologize, and start fresh.

I once read about a tribe that, when someone offended within the tribe, would place the errant member within a circle of all the people of the tribe. Then, one by one, they would each tell the misbehaver good things about themselves until the wrongdoer shifted their attitude and responded back to the tribe with love. They said this was rarely necessary, but it almost always worked to correct the person's behavior. I wonder what our "civilized" society would be like if we responded more to each other with love than condemnation? Happy people are not rude, cruel, or violent. We can't make others be happy, but we can be kind and we can intend to act with love. This is the magic alchemy that heals relationships.

Above all, be true to yourself and to the people that you choose relationships with. Share your authentic self in a kind manner and your relationships will bless you and everyone else in your life.

Thank you for taking the time to spend in the vibration of this material. May you, and all of your relationships, be filled with bliss.

Random Resource I Love for Improving Relationships:

The Vortex: Where the Law of Attraction Assembles All Cooperative Relationships, by Esther and Jerry Hicks

LOA for Love, by Jeannette Maw (can be found at www.goodvibeblog.com)

The Five Love Languages, by Gary Chapman

Light His Fire and *Light Her Fire*, by Dr. Ellen Kreidman

Magnificent...Married or Not: Reaching your Highest Self Before, During, and After Divorce, by Cloris Kylie

Communication Miracles for Couples: Easy and Effective Ways to Have More Love and Less Conflict, by Jonathan Robinson

To Love Is To Be Happy With, by Barry Neil Kaufman

If I Have To Tell You One More Time...: The Revolutionary Program That Gets Your Kids To Listen Without Nagging, Reminding, or Yelling by Amy McReady

Liberated Parents, Liberated Children: Your Guide to a Happier Family, by Adele Faber, Elaine Mazlish and Kimberly Ann Coe (I love all Adele and Elaine's books.)

1001 Ways to be Romantic, by Gregory Godek

Heal Your Family Karma, by Sara Wiseman

Animal-Speak: The Spiritual & Magical Powers of Creatures Great & Small, by Ted Andrews

Coaches, Experiences, and Programs

Amy Flynn: Generational Healing. Clear generations of resistant emotional energy and blocks permanently, with a trapped emotional energy clearing session. EnergyClearing.wealthabundancejoynow.com

The Art of Love and Sex Tantra Online Course by Lola Jones on www.divineopenings.com

Coach Lisa Hayes, The Love Whisperer at www.lisamhayes.com

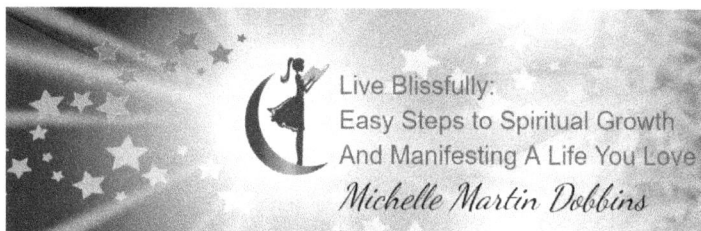

Live Blissfully:
Easy Steps to Spiritual Growth
And Manifesting A Life You Love
Michelle Martin Dobbins

Freebies Only for the Readers of Relationship Alchemy

Thank you for purchasing my book, *Relationship Alchemy*, and taking the time to read it!

May you discover some tips that help you find more joy and love in your life.

Sign up to receive all the free audios mentioned in the book.

- What is the Difference Between Alchemy and Law of Attraction?
- Family DNA Vibe Healing
- The Friendship Vortex
- Connecting With Others' Higher Selves
- How I Almost Instantly Manifested a Man
- Vibe Mixology for Love Relationships
- Cutting Relationship Cords
- The Magic Bubble
- Seeing the Beauty in Everyone

dailyalchemy.com/relationship-alchemy

Acknowledgments

I could never have completed this book without many wonderful people supporting me. First, I want to thank my parents, Velma and Merel Martin, for loving me and allowing me to be myself, even though my own personality is quite different than theirs. It's so much easier to follow your own path when you have that unconditional support from birth.

Thanks to Rozlyn Warren for making sure that no mistakes snuck through.

Thanks to my family. My husband, David Dobbins, has always encouraged me to follow my dreams and has tolerated lots of nights listening to me typing while he tried to sleep. Serenity, my oldest daughter, gives me wonderful critiques and encouragement. Her younger siblings, Kadin, Kali, and Violet are the best fans any writer could have. They love to tell people that their mommy is a writer, and that fortifies me to not give up. Big love to all the members of my family tree: past, present and future. Thank you for the collective energy you bring to my life.

Special thanks to Tiffany Smallwood for supporting my writing above and beyond what I would expect of any friend.

I am truly very blessed by all the wonderful people who support me. Thanks to all of you who have encouraged me and let me know that my words touched you. It means to world to me. Thank you all.

~Michelle Martin Dobbins

About The Author

Michelle Martin Dobbins is an author, spiritual alchemist & reiki master who shares true stories of magic, creation and love in everyday life at dailyalchemy.com. She adores reading, writing, meditating, homeschooling her four children and supporting people to transform their lives using love and joy... Oh, and chocolate. Lots of chocolate.

Connect with Michelle:

- MichelleDobbinsAuthor
- @MichelleDobbins
- MichelleMartinDobbins
- MichelleMartinDobbins
- DMDobbins98